JOE POLLACK'S
GUIDE TO
ST. LOUIS RESTAURANTS

Second Edition

CHICAGO
REVIEW
PRESS

Library of Congress Cataloging-in-Publication Data

Pollack, Joe.
  [Guide to St. Louis restaurants]
  Joe Pollack's guide to St. Louis restaurants. —2nd ed.
    p. cm.
  Includes indexes.
  ISBN 1-55652-144-8 : $9.95
  1. Restaurants, lunch rooms, etc.—Missouri—St. Louis
Region—Guidebooks. I. Title. II. Title: Guide to St. Louis res-
taurants. III. Title: Joe Pollack's guide to St. Louis restaurants.
  TX907.3.M82S26 1992
  647.95778'66—dc20   92-3382
                                          CIP

Cover Painting: Jane Fisher, *Oriental Fan*, 1986, oil on canvas, 36" x 54". Courtesy of Struve Gallery, Chicago, Illinois.

1 2 3 4 5 6 7 8 9 10

Published in 1992 by Chicago Review Press, Incorporated
814 North Franklin Street, Chicago, Illinois 60610
ISBN 1-55652-144-8

To Wendy, Dara, and Sharon, with hope that they and their children will make the twenty-first century better than the twentieth. To Mom. And, of course, to Carol, the constant and cheerful fellow-traveler on these gastronomic journeys.

Contents

Introduction

❖❖❖

I might have made a mistake.

Four years ago, for the first edition of this book, I wrote the introduction first. Looking back, it might have been the wrong way to go about it, because after making a series of wide-ranging judgments, I then wrote about the individual restaurants. It might have been backward.

But we'll find out. This time, after writing all the individual sketches, it's time for the introduction. I think I may have a better perspective.

In those four years, a lot has happened. Two dozen restaurants that were discussed in the first edition, some very favorably, have vanished. Interestingly, showing the basic optimism of the restaurateur, more than that have arrived.

Several others opened and seemed headed for these pages, then closed—victims of the recession, of insufficient capitalization, of incompetence, of bad luck, and any number of other reasons.

So where do we stand?

Four years ago, I wrote lovingly of the so-called class of '72, the five restaurants that changed St. Louis dining that year. Today, only two (Balaban's and Duff's) continue strong. Two others (Anthony's and Richard Perry) have closed, and the fifth (Yen Ching), mired in its 20-year-old culinary style, didn't qualify.

But there's a raft of new places to carry on to reach new heights—Cafe Zoe made the move from Lafayette Square to Clayton, went full-time at dinner, and is a delight. Cardwell's displayed hearty American cooking and became an immediate success. David Guempel left Balaban's, opened Zinnia, and brought elegant dining to Webster Groves. Grappa, operated by two men who had trained at Cardwell's, joined the Central West End's hip crowd. Tim Mallett and the Blue Water Grill carried Southwestern-Mexican cuisine to Hampton Avenue.

Vietnamese cooking arrived in a string of small, delicate spots on South Grand Boulevard, and the Royal Chinese Barbecue gave

1

Olive Street Road a San Francisco look by hanging barbecued ducks in the window. The University City Loop became more fun than ever, with an impressive lineup of ethnic restaurants along Delmar from Skinker to Kingsland. Tom Sehnert took his great, home-smoked meats from the case at the Smoke House and began serving them next door at Annie Gunn's.

Kemoll's was another restaurant to move, from the North Side to Downtown, and to busy times in the Metropolitan Square Building. Dominic's and Mineo's opened downtown branches, though the latter failed to survive 1991. Giovanni's from the Hill and Agostino's Colosseum put their sons in charge of new operations, as did Franco's from Belleville.

Old favorite restaurants, and top chefs, continued to grow and glow. Marcel Keraval (Cafe de France), Al Baroni (Al's Steak House), Fio Antognini (Fio's La Fourchette), Dominic Galati (Dominic's), and Andy Ayers (Riddle's) remained in the top echelon while younger men like Rich LoRusso (LoRusso's) and John Vitale (Gino's) made their marks, along with many of those listed above. If I inadvertently overlooked anyone, my apologies.

A major 1992 change will see Tony's, the standard by which all St. Louis restaurants are judged, move from the only space it's ever known to new quarters, with no stairs to climb, nine blocks to the south. Vince Bommarito, enthused by the challenge, insists the new establishment will be better than ever, and I'm sure he also sees it as his legacy to Vince Jr., who keeps growing in stature and ability, both in the kitchen and in the front of the house.

While we have many good restaurants, and can still stand tall among American cities, with the exception of the Big Six—New York, Washington, Chicago, New Orleans, San Francisco, and Los Angeles—it doesn't mean everything is perfect. We still need an elegant Chinese seafood restaurant in the Cantonese-Shanghai style, and we lack Eastern European, Spanish, and Caribbean cuisine. Our Mexican and German restaurants fall short, too.

The city's advances in the last four years are in American cuisine of various types, in some experimental dishes, and in the use of game. Our French and Italian restaurants can stand against any in the nation. Wine lists have continued to grow, and moderately priced, well-made wines are available in most restaurants. Several feature Missouri wines, which also have made noble growth in the last decade, and more St. Louis diners should try them. The surprise will be pleasant.

Our other strong point is in small, informal restaurants for lunch, places for a hearty sandwich and a bowl of good soup. We have many, all over the area.

I find it difficult to believe, but I've now been dining professionally in St. Louis for 20 years, and eating heartily for seventeen before that. It's been fun all the way, and to paraphrase one of my favorite local hosts, I hope you enjoy reading this book as much as I did writing it.

P.S.—We're now starting to export chefs and restaurateurs, and they are receiving outstanding notices in the national media.

David Slay took his La Veranda to Los Angeles, and last year it was rated the best new restaurant in Beverly Hills. Slay is doing some of the same things he did here, and many more, in an informal setting. I've eaten there, and it's superb.

Danny Meyer, who grew up in St. Louis and whose late father was in the restaurant business, has the Union Square Cafe in New York, one of the very best in the city. There are Italian overtones to a menu that is wide-ranging, and he has several Missouri wines on his excellent list.

As long as we're traveling, let me add a few other personal favorites—the Frontera Grill in Chicago, Emeril in New Orleans, and Stars in San Francisco.

How To Use This Guide

Since the first edition of this book was published nearly four years ago, a few things have changed, and others have remained the same.

I've added a second restaurant article each week, a "Business Lunch" piece for the Business Plus tabloid that runs in the *Post-Dispatch* every Monday. It's shorter and not quite as serious as the regular Thursday review, providing me a little more opportunity to tell stories, and while it primarily deals with smaller, lunch-type places, I've also visited the more elegant spots. Overall, it has given me a chance to learn more about the local eating routine.

The fact that the earth travels around the sun, aside from any personal skill, has increased my experience to nearly twenty years of restaurant writing, and more than one thousand articles.

What has not changed are the same irrefutable facts I listed here in the first edition:

1. Restaurants set their own standards for being judged.
2. Being recognized as a restaurant writer is no guarantee of better dining.

Let me explain the second point first. Unless you're a master of disguise, it's impossible to remain anonymous for very long. The facts that I was rather visible in the community long before I took this job, and that I appear on television, are certainly important. Equally important, however, is the fact that bartenders and serving personnel are very transient, and good bartenders have good memories for faces.

And then there are friends, acquaintances, and neighbors. For example, I go to dinner. Across the room, someone I met at a party the previous weekend recognizes me. The odds are heavy that he (or she) will show off some knowledge and ask the waiter, "Do you know who that is, eating at that table over there?"

In addition, much of the restaurant's work for tonight's dinner was complete long before the first diner arrived. Raw materials were ordered and delivered, roasts were cooked, sauces made, soups stirred, and salad dressings mixed. There isn't much more that can be done at that point. I take precautions to always make reservations in another name, so no one knows I'm there until I walk in, and I try to order from the menu, rather than from the specials, though there are exceptions. I also try to let the restaurant take its best shot; in other words, if the menu notes that any certain item is a specialty, I'll order it.

The statement that restaurants set their own standards for being judged may sound rather arbitrary, but judging restaurants became a lot easier, and more logical, when I realized it. I also realized that I'd been doing it all along, without conscious thought.

When you spend $125 for dinner for two, you expect a great deal more than if you spend $30. I do, and I judge accordingly. There are no minor mistakes at the high end of the scale. All errors are major errors.

When a restaurateur tells me, via the menu, that he has the most expensive restaurant in town, he's also telling me—whether he wants to or not—that he has the best restaurant in town. Then my years in Missouri come to the fore, and he has to show me.

The recognition factor can affect service, but I've been doing this long enough to recognize it. It's unfortunate when serving personnel become intimidated or work on the edge of panic, but it happens. In general, the waiters and waitresses of St. Louis are a competent, highly professional group, and it's rare that service falters.

One other kind word for St. Louis restaurants—through all the years and thousands of meals, I have never become ill. I've overeaten to the point of discomfort, but that's my fault, not the chef's.

I'm lucky enough to like just about everything that restaurants serve. Despite occasional disparagement, I even like broccoli, cauliflower, and zucchini, if they're properly prepared and not an everyday occurrence. Carrots are nearing that overused territory as they seem to be more and more popular, even in Chinese restaurants (maybe especially in Chinese restaurants).

I wish St. Louis restaurants were more adventuresome in their vegetables; I like beets, and braised celery, and leeks, and spinach, and beet greens, and even brussels sprouts.

I like organ meats like liver, sweetbreads, and kidneys, and I'm weak for clams on the half-shell, sushi, and steak tartar. I like my beef rare and I've reached the point where I like salmon, swordfish, and duck rare in the middle. I like salads, especially when they're tossed tableside, and I don't like them drowned in dressing. I don't like pasta drowned in sauce either. I'm weak when it comes to Asian cuisine, especially the spicy variety, and I'm probably most charitable toward those restaurants.

5

For a single meal, I would go to a haute-cuisine French restaurant, but I never met an ethnic restaurant I wouldn't try. I want to taste the raw material under the sauce, and I want spicy dishes to have a distinct pop, but not a severe burn. I like hot dogs and junk food.

When it comes to wine, I prefer hearty, full-bodied reds, either French or California, but I like some of the Italian reds, too. Most Americans prefer white wines, and I try to make sure they're properly represented.

I get angry when restaurant wine lists do not include vintages, or when the list shows one date and the bottle another. I get angrier when there is no wine list at all, just some unknown stuff by the glass. There is enough modestly priced wine out there that any restaurant, no matter how small, should have six or eight wines available by the bottle, half that many by the glass.

Wine markup in a restaurant should result in a price that is about twice retail. More than that borders on outrageous, less than that is to be commended highly. I'm disturbed by the fact that a number of restaurants quietly add the tax, a fact you don't notice until the bill arrives.

The commentary in this book should be self-explanatory. I don't like cutesy codes or fancy symbols, and I've never understood how some people can rate one wine a 93 and another a 92. Given changes in the last four years, I've adjusted the price codes to match. Under $15 is now "inexpensive," $15–$25 is "moderate," $25–$35 is "expensive," and over $35 is "very expensive." That includes an appetizer or salad (if the salad is à la carte), entree, and dessert for one. It does not include drinks, tax, or tip.

And to repeat: Over the years, I always have described myself as a literate person of strong opinions. I know the latter characteristic will come through on these pages. I hope the former does, too.

Prices are as of late 1991; there are no guarantees that they will not rise or that chefs will not move. After all, there is no free lunch.

6

DOWNTOWN

Includes Laclede's Landing and nearby restaurant areas like Lafayette Square, Soulard, and the Union Station restaurant-entertainment-shopping complex.

Al's Steak House
Amighetti's Bakery (see Hill Listings)
Arcelia's (Soulard)
Boston Seafood Restaurant (Union Station)
Cafe de France
Catfish & Crystal (see Miss Hulling's)
Charlie Gitto's Pasta House
Crown Candy Kitchen (North)
Dierdorf & Hart's (Union Station)
1860 Hard Shell Cafe (Soulard)
Faust's (Adam's Mark Hotel)
Houlihan's (Union Station)
J. F. Sanfilippo's
J. W. Carver's (Marriott Hotel)
Jack Carl's Two Cents Plain
John D. McGurk's Irish Pub (Soulard)
Kemoll's
Kennedy's Second Street Company (Laclede's Landing)
Key West Cafe (Union Station)

Lt. Robert E. Lee
Lucius Boomer (Laclede's Landing)
McMurphy's
Mike & Min's (Soulard)
Mike Shannon's Steaks and Seafood
Miss Hulling's Cafeteria (with Catfish & Crystal)
The Ninth & Russell (Soulard)
O. T. Hodge Chili Parlor
Park Avenue Cafe (Lafayette Square)
Premio
Ruth's Chris Steak House
Sidney Street Cafe (Soulard)
The Station Grille (Hyatt Hotel, Union Station)
The Tap Room
Tony's
Top of the Riverfront (Clarion Hotel)
Tucker's Place (Soulard)

AL'S STEAK HOUSE
1200 North Main St.
(1st and Biddle)
421-6399

❖❖

Cuisine: Steaks, chops, seafood, Italian accents
Serves: Dinner only, Monday–Saturday
Prices: Very expensive
Credit Cards: MC, V
Dress: Restaurant formal (jacket and tie for men)
Reservations: Accepted and advised
Handicap Access: Satisfactory
Separate No-Smoking Section: No

When Italian immigrants came to St. Louis in the late 19th century, they didn't all settle on the Hill. Many lived in a downtown enclave, including the Baronis, who had a grocery store and lived above it. In 1925, it became a restaurant, with a cafeteria line for lunch, red-checked tablecloths, and pasta in the evenings.

Over the years, and through several remodelings—one caused by a fire—Al Baroni converted it into an elegant establishment, in a low-key, dark-paneled room with comfortable chairs at large tables.

And the dining experience can be outstanding, with huge portions of perfect steaks and chops and seafood, served in superior style. Techniques of preparation can range from simple to complex; the old-fashioned trencherman (or woman) will be more than satisfied.

Al's does not offer a printed menu, a fact I have deplored from time to time, but an experienced and talented waiter brings a silver tray with a display of the evening's offerings: burly steaks, beautifully marbled and perfectly trimmed; handsome lamb chops; huge chops and pale medallions of veal for sautéing and saucing; plus

8

several fish and chicken selections. The mind may be boggled after the presentation, however, because there are sauces to consider and often variations on cooking procedures as well.

As mentioned, there are Italian overtones, with some superior pastas as appetizers or side dishes, along with shrimp de Jonghe, scallops, and escargot.

Salads, either tossed green, Caesar, or spinach, also are highlights; but appetizer, salad, entree, and dessert are just too much dinner. Three out of four are usually on the high end of sufficiency. Over the years, I've found the meat entrees to be the highlights at Al's. Sirloin steaks are perfect, whether broiled as is, or nicely peppered; and lamb, in rack or chops, is special when marinated and barely brushed with seasoned bread crumbs. Veal piccata, the meat sautéd in wine and lemon juice, is simple and delightful, and the mammoth veal chop is something to see—and to eat.

Al's also makes an art of the simple potato; whether hash-browned, cottage-fried, or baked, they're splendid. Spinach, eggplant, and other vegetables are expertly prepared, and a side order of cappellini pasta, in butter and garlic, is also a winner.

The wine list is long, outstanding, and expensive, with some of the finest French, Italian, and California vintages. Dessert is also displayed on a tray and is a fitting finale featuring numerous winners, but after dinner at Al's, a brandy or Armagnac or Calvados with coffee is usually just right.

ARCELIA'S
2501 South Ninth St.
(Soulard)
776-5900

❖❖

Cuisine: Mexican
Serves: Breakfast, lunch, and dinner, every day
Prices: Inexpensive
Credit Cards: MC, V
Dress: Casual
Reservations: Only for parties of six or more
Handicap Access: Passable, with some difficulty
Separate No-Smoking Section: No

St. Louis diners get short shrift when it comes to Mexican food. We have a number of Mexican restaurants, but only a few are worth visiting, and those are too far from downtown. But now Arcelia's has arrived in the southern part of the Soulard area, almost within the shadow of Anheuser-Busch. Despite their location, they don't have a liquor license, so bring your own beer.

Authentic Mexican dishes, along with those that are mostly Americanized, come hot and tasty from the kitchen in the small, crowded place where those who wait fill a small doorway or use the sidewalk.

Red and green salsa accompany fresh, warm, slightly greasy chips, and while the red salsa strikes sparks, the green can ignite a full-fledged conflagration. Menudo, the thick Mexican soup made with tripe, often is available, as is pozole, another soup with full-sized hominy, plus fresh onions and cabbage served alongside for tossing into the bowl.

Guacamole, thick and lumpy and tasting of avocado and not mayonnaise, is delicious, as is quesofundido, a white cheese melted over tangy chorizo.

There are hard and soft tacos, corn and flour enchiladas (when a Mexican menu says "flour," it means wheat flour; "corn" is corn), burritos and chalupas filled with beef or chicken or cheese, and everything sings. Flautas, or deep-fried tortillas, are splendid, and delicious beans come alongside, improved by a hit of green salsa.

Save room for a sopapilla too, big as a softball and light as a feather; the dough simply melts in your mouth. Buñuelos and flan are available too, but they don't hold a candle to the sopapillas.

I keep meaning to sample the breakfast at Arcelia's, but my metabolism just doesn't get me moving early enough in the morning.

BOSTON SEAFOOD RESTAURANT
Union Station, Market Street, 18th to 20th Streets
621-3474

Cuisine: Seafood
Serves: Lunch and dinner, every day
Prices: Moderate to expensive
Credit Cards: All major
Dress: Informal
Reservations: Accepted
Handicap Access: Satisfactory
Separate No-Smoking Section: Yes

Boston Seafood Restaurant, once the Boston Seafood Company, is on the second floor of the Union Station complex, tucked neatly into a corner where a patio area offers outdoor dining in those months when the weather is acceptable. It overlooks a pond, and some trains, a view not to be compared with a roaring surf, but pleasant enough.

Seafood is the specialty, with first-rate oysters and clams on the half-shell and some lobster specials which are usually a good value. The nonseafood eater will find some steaks and chops.

In addition to the raw crustaceans, the appetizer list includes gumbo, Cajun shrimp, and steamed mussels. The gumbo needs more spicing, and perhaps some okra, and the mussels need less cooking. An order I tried was tired, tough, and tasteless.

The same inconsistency was displayed in entrees—with excellent catfish and salmon, and unsatisfactory scallops and shrimp. French fries and slaw were proper accompaniments, but the baked potatoes were variable.

The wine list had some pleasant selections at moderate prices, and dessert, highlighted by a chocolate mousse cake, was delightful.

12

CAFE DE FRANCE
410 Olive Street
231-2204

❖❖

Cuisine: French
Serves: Dinner, Monday–Saturday
Prices: Very expensive
Credit Cards: All major
Dress: Restaurant formal (jackets for men)
Reservations: Accepted and advised
Handicap Access: Satisfactory
Separate No-Smoking Section: No

The great trinity of the kitchen—love, talent, and imagination—is always present here, where Owner-Chef Marcel Keraval stands guard over a downtown jewel that is as fine an example of haute cuisine French cooking as this city possesses. In classic French style, his wife, Monique, is in the front of the house, welcoming guests to the small, perfectly lighted room.

It is a place for dinner and romance in the grand tradition, and the chef does not disappoint. It's expensive, whether by tasting menu or on an à la carte basis, but dinner at Cafe de France is for special events, and it's been a long time since anything I tasted there was less than outstanding.

Classic service goes with classic cooking, and from the first taste of home-baked, crusty bread to the final bite of a flawless soufflé or fruit tart, Cafe de France provides elegance and delicacy on the plate and on the palate.

Sauces are not as rich and buttery as they once were, but the word *nouvelle* doesn't fit here. Rich stocks and an ideal touch with spices and herbs, plus top-quality materials, are always in evidence. Oysters from the coast of Maine or the Pacific Northwest are available in season, and Keraval serves them with a basic vinaigrette and shallot sauce for dipping. No ketchup and horseradish for these tasty beauties.

Quail pâté, served warm and en croute, is another rich and delicate dish, and Keraval prepares escargot en croute, too, with much evidence of garlic, and pastry that simply melts in the mouth. Soups are rich and tasty, and always just right for the season, and a fish soup one night brought back memories of well-remembered visits to Keraval's native country.

Traditional fowl is much in evidence and always perfectly prepared. And both the cherry and the orange sauce do magic things with duck. Stuffed quail was a melt-in-the-mouth delight one night, with a nicely spiced dressing that was a perfect complement to the tender, delicious birds. But Cafe de France also does brilliant things with venison, and a tender, delicious filet had just the barest hint of gaminess, just enough to give it distinction. Fresh cranberries came alongside, plus a large handful of morel mushrooms, for a perfect combination.

Fresh fish, sautéd in a variety of ways, is always on the menu, and frog legs, large and tender and prepared with lots of garlic and tomato in the Provençal style, are another fine choice.

For the meat lover, there are steaks, or tournedos, or lamb chops, all prepared to the moment and served with a sauce to match. The Bearnaise is especially good.

Vegetables of the season, always fresh and always nicely prepared, come alongside—in presentation that emphasizes both their colors and delicacy.

The Cafe de France wine list is as strong as a top restaurant merits, and there are some fine California labels to go along with a wide French assortment.

Keraval is a brilliant pastry chef, and the cart is a thing of beauty, both to view and to taste. His classic Grand Marnier soufflé, with sabayon sauce, is hard to resist. Only a tea drinker was disappointed—and so was I—when, in a restaurant of this class, the tea came from a bag emblazoned with the name Lipton.

CHARLIE GITTO'S PASTA HOUSE
207 North Sixth St.
436-2828

◆◆◆

Cuisine: Italian
Serves: Lunch and dinner, Monday–Saturday
Prices: Moderate
Credit Cards: All major
Dress: Casual
Reservations: Accepted
Handicap Access: Satisfactory
Separate No-Smoking Section: No

A spin-off of the more elegant Gitto's on the Hill, this downtown pasta house provides moderately priced, filling, satisfying standard pasta and Italian fare. Its proximity to Busch Stadium, as well as the prices and portions, attract the sports crowd. Tommy Lasorda, the Dodgers' manager, is a regular customer, though he now seems to prefer the diet foods he sponsors to Gitto's pasta.

Busy and popular, Gitto's offers satisfactory toasted ravioli, and salads are large and fresh. Pastas include cavatelli, linguine, canneloni, lasagna, and many other shapes, and are topped with a wide variety of sauces. I'm fond of the linguine with clam sauce, and there's good garlic bread for mopping the plate.

Pasta houses like Gitto's have proliferated here in the last decade or so, and the secret to their success is simple—satisfactory meals at moderate prices.

CROWN CANDY KITCHEN
1401 St. Louis Ave.
621-9650

❖❖❖

Cuisine: Ice cream, sodas, malts, sundaes, and sandwiches
Serves: Lunchtime until after-dinner dessert, every day
Prices: Inexpensive
Credit Cards: Not applicable
Dress: Casual
Reservations: For ice cream cones?
Handicap Access: Satisfactory
Separate No-Smoking Section: No

A real St. Louis classic, the Crown Candy Kitchen has been serving smiles since it opened in 1913. A wonderful, old-fashioned soda fountain and candy store on the northern edge of downtown, it's a step through a time warp to the soda fountains of the 1930s, when carbonated water came out of a fountain tap, sodas were built in tall glasses, and those ageless teenagers, the Coca-Cola kids, smiled down from their frames on the walls.

They make their own candy and ice cream in this friendly place that has survived several fires and a changing neighborhood but has retained its integrity and charm, complete to small booths with those old-fashioned jukebox players hanging from their walls.

Ice cream is excellent and rich, led by fresh peach in summer. My current favorite is chocolate-chocolate chip, a treat for the lover of dark chocolate. More important, everything is prepared by hand, in the old-fashioned way. To make a soda, syrup is carefully stirred by hand into the bottom of a tall glass, and carbonated water is added slowly and carefully for the proper foamy top. Whipped cream is optional.

Malts and milk shakes are made in metal containers, and when the thick, sluggish semiliquid is poured into the glass, a little

16

remains in the container and both go to the table for an extra treat, what they call a "lagniappe" in New Orleans. Sundaes arrive in tulip glasses, with towers of fruit or fudge, heaps of nuts, and mounds of whipped cream.

As an extra bonus, several generations of New Yorkers have taught the St. Louis–born owners how to prepare a most satisfactory egg cream.

If you can't justify an all-ice-cream lunch, there are sandwiches too, on old-fashioned white toast, providing perfectly satisfactory tuna fish, chicken salads, BLT's and the like.

The Crown is only 5 to 10 minutes from downtown and draws as many coat-and-tie customers for lunch as it does anything else. You'd be surprised at the corporate types who sneak away for some ice cream. And on weekends, this is a place for parents and grandparents to show the little ones some of the very best parts of the good old days.

DIERDORF & HART'S

Union Station 421-1772

West Port Plaza 878-1801

✦✦

Cuisine: Steaks, chops, and seafood
Serves: Lunch and dinner, every day
Prices: Expensive, sometimes very expensive
Credit Cards: All major
Dress: Informal
Reservations: Accepted
Handicap Access: Satisfactory
Separate No-Smoking Section: Yes

Unlike those in many cities, St. Louis–based athletes have never been major restaurant promoters until recently. For many years, only Stan Musial was involved, but after he gave up greeting and glad-handing, the field lay fallow for a number of years.

Former NFL standouts Dan Dierdorf and Jim Hart changed that with a pair of steak houses, first in West Port Plaza in the west county, then at the renovated Union Station downtown. Dierdorf, a perennial all-pro offensive tackle and one of the best ever at the position, now is an ABC commentator on "Monday Night Football"; Hart, a very talented but underappreciated quarterback, now is athletic director at Southern Illinois University in Carbondale.

Mike Shannon, baseball Cardinal third baseman and now a broadcaster, has a downtown steak house, too, and Blues' hockey player Brett Hull lent his name to a 1991 rookie in the far west county. Both restaurants are operated by the Pasta House Company. The Chicago interests who have Mike Ditka's restaurant there tried here with Whitey Herzog, but it was a flop.

Both Dierdorf-Hart spots, old-fashioned chophouses in the classic style, provide superior steaks from huge cuts of beef, nicely marbled and properly prepared. Porterhouse, T-bone, sirloin, filet, arrive in sizes that could be described as large, monster, and oh-my-goodness, and if a 32-ounce porterhouse or 24-ounce T-bone won't fill you, nothing will.

Entrees are displayed on a silver tray and nicely described by the waiter, but a menu also is provided.

Although the steaks are good and perfectly cooked, other things have been rather ordinary and often carelessly prepared. Vegetables have been cool or half hot, half cold. Other entrees, like lamb and veal chops, are satisfactory, while fish dishes tend to be not much more than passable.

Salads are fresh and tasty, and D & H serves a traditional New York chophouse salad of a chilled wedge of iceberg lettuce. It's a nice change.

Among appetizers, fresh oysters and clams casino have been the most successful.

The wine list is large and elegant, strong on reds, with some outstanding entries from both France and California. Desserts are ordinary.

1860 HARD SHELL CAFE
1860 South Ninth St.
231-1860

✦━✦

Cuisine: American, with Cajun overtones
Serves: Lunch and dinner, every day
Prices: Inexpensive to moderate
Credit Cards: MC, V
Dress: Casual
Reservations: Accepted
Handicap Access: Satisfactory
Separate No-Smoking Section: No

The Soulard neighborhood, about 10 minutes south of downtown, is a lovely area of rehabbed houses and old-fashioned bars and restaurants, many with fireplaces and exposed brick. Live music is a regular occurrence, there are occasional poetry readings, and the aura is always relaxed.

The 1860, named for its address, has high ceilings, a large fireplace, and some superior seafood dishes at moderate prices. There are Cajun overtones here and there, and some New Orleans dishes like shrimp étouffée, gumbo, and red beans and rice. The latter two dishes were exemplary.

In addition, there's a splendid T-bone steak; the one I sampled was as good as any I've experienced, with flavor and tenderness of the highest level.

On the other hand, I was disappointed to learn that only filets of catfish were available, and not the whole fish, such a delight when properly battered with cornmeal and then fried. In general, the grilled dishes are superior to the fried ones.

The wine list is small but offers some good choices, and homemade pies (especially pumpkin) are outstanding.

FAUST'S
Adam's Mark Hotel
4th & Chestnut Streets
342-4690

✧✧

Cuisine: Modern American, with French overtones
Serves: Lunch, Monday–Friday; dinner, every evening
Prices: Expensive to very expensive
Credit Cards: All major
Dress: Jacket preferred
Reservations: Accepted and advised
Handicap Access: Satisfactory
Separate No-Smoking Section: Yes

Although its name goes back to the turn of the century, when the original Tony Faust's was one of the great American restaurants, there's nothing old-fashioned about the contemporary version. It's the sort of hotel dining room that more hotels should have, with elegance and haute cuisine to show off the best of the city and the best of downtown.

The ground-floor room is one of the loveliest in the area, with a rear section that overlooks the Arch grounds. The imaginative menu blends the best of Modern American, with fresh ingredients for items that are usually grilled and lightly sauced, with some classic dishes and cooking methods showing a solid French influence.

As a result, the Adam's Mark and Faust's are in step with the most-welcome trend that sees hotel restaurants once again becoming places that serve superior meals. These places are now drawing city residents in search of excellence and not just hotel guests without dining options.

Faust's is a large, softly lighted room with spacious tables, comfortable chairs, and plenty of room between dining parties.

Service is excellent, and the wine service matches, or exceeds, any place in the city.

Herbs and spices are used intelligently and imaginatively, and in winter game is often featured. Venison, quail, and wild hare have all been featured on the menu. Grilled venison was outstanding, with the meat showing all the dark richness that it can possibly display.

A ragout of hare was a delightful appetizer, served on a bed of spinach in a sauce that included raisins. On the simpler side, lobster bisque was rich and delicious, and a chunk of fresh salmon was perfectly poached, with a hint of ginger in a light sauce adding a superb touch.

The trend of filling ravioli with more than Italian sausage or ground beef is shown here too, and a lobster-scallop blend was perfect, in homemade pasta that was light and perfectly cooked, slightly chewy but not tough.

Classic appetizers like steak tartar are superior, and there's more to fresh fish than the salmon, as shown in a perfectly grilled sea bass. Duck has been a success on every occasion, and even the baby vegetables are nicely cooked. Presentation is usually outstanding, though it sometimes errs on the side of being overbusy.

Salads feature fresh, delicious greens and a lovely, light vinaigrette dressing. The wine list is excellent, with domestic and imported bottles representing the finest regions and vintages, and most prices showing a reasonable markup.

Fresh fruit in season and a beautiful pastry tray lead the dessert selections. The classic fruit tart arrives looking and tasting just as it should, and the chocolate shavings on top of the chocolate mousse cake are as large as roof shingles—and boy, are they ever delicious.

HOULIHAN'S

Union Station **436-0844**
Galleria **863-9116**
West County Center **821-0900**

‹›

Cuisine: American Trendy
Serves: Lunch and dinner, every day; brunch on Sundays
Prices: Moderate
Credit Cards: All major
Dress: Casual
Reservations: Accepted
Handicap Access: Satisfactory
Separate No-Smoking Section: Yes

With two locations in suburban shopping malls and a third in the rehabbed Union Station, these are always crowded, always busy bars that also serve food, ever the trendiest and never the best.

That doesn't seem to deter those who hang out here, amid the noise, telling the latest jokes, and sampling the latest in drinks.

Lunch is generally acceptable, and at dinner times it can be a passable place for grazing among the appetizers.

23

J. F. SANFILIPPO'S
705 North Broadway
621-7213

•>

Cuisine: Italian
Serves: Lunch and dinner, every day
Prices: Moderate
Credit Cards: All major
Dress: Informal
Reservations: Accepted
Handicap Access: Satisfactory
Separate No-Smoking Section: No

Another of the growing group of second-generation Italian restaurateurs and chefs is J. F. Sanfilippo, whose parents, Franco and Concetta, operate Franco's, long an East Side favorite. The cord isn't quite cut yet either, as Mrs. Sanfilippo is still on hand to run the ovens—producing wondrous breads and pastries.

Her dinner rolls, sometimes stuffed with ham and cheese, sometimes just poppy-seed-covered and crunchy on the outside, soft and delicious on the inside, are glorious, and her cannoli and other desserts are as good as can be found in the city.

The cuisine is Italian, mainly Sicilian, with a splendid collection of pastas. Rigatoni, canneloni, fettuccine, cavatelli, and other noodles lead the way, under a variety of sauces. I'm a big fan of rigatoni, a thick, ridged pasta that takes sauces very well and doesn't drip on my shirt. Cooked "alla matriciana," with tomato, bacon, onion and white wine, it's a delight.

Eggplant Parmigiana is a splendid appetizer, and other fine entrees include veal Franco—a good veal tournedo topped with cheese and a slice of ham.

Pasta side dishes complement the entrees nicely, and so does steamed fresh spinach topped with pimento. The dinner salads are crisp and nicely topped with a good oil-and-vinegar dressing.

The wine list is modest, but there are hearty reds to accompany the hearty pasta.

Save room for Concetta Sanfilippo's desserts, even beyond the cannoli. There's also an excellent apple-caramel-brandy pie, with Granny Smith apples for tart, caramel for sweet, and brandy for just a little bite. Excellent.

J. W. CARVER'S
Marriott Pavilion Hotel
Broadway and Market Streets
421-1776

❖❖

Cuisine: Basic American steaks, chops, and seafood
Serves: Dinner, Monday–Saturday; lunch, Monday–Friday
Prices: Expensive
Credit Cards: All major
Dress: Informal
Reservations: Accepted and advised
Handicap Access: Satisfactory
Separate No-Smoking Section: Yes

Like all mayors of St. Louis, before or after, the late A. J. Cervantes did a few silly things, like bringing a replica of the Santa Maria to the Riverfront. But he did some outstanding things too, like convincing St. Louisans we wanted to bring the Spanish Pavilion, lock, stock, and tiles, from the New York World's Fair of 1964 to be a centerpiece of downtown.

Lots of children, including mine, kicked in their pennies and nickels, and one day it arrived. Unfortunately it did not succeed as a meeting place, theater, and restaurant complex, as planned, and a Marriott Hotel was built above it. Today, only the tile lobby floor remains to jog old-timers' memories, but the Pavilion, and the hotel, and the stadium across the street, did spark a revival downtown.

But off in a quiet corner, in a softly lighted room, J. W. Carver's offers first-rate fare of basic American steaks, chops, and prime rib, all well prepared and nicely presented. There are a handful of seafood specials, and a few other dishes as well, but the basics are the Carver strong suit, and all have been excellent. Prime rib, for example, is a worthy selection, and so are the steaks, and Carver's presents baked potatoes that are delicious and foilless.

Beef Wellington is delicious, with a light flaky crust, and fresh fish is perfectly broiled.

Appetizers include the simple shrimp cocktail, and a first-rate coquilles St. Jacques that consists of delicious scallops and tasty mashed potatoes, all nicely browned in a delicate sauce. Lobster bisque is exemplary, with chunks of lobster adding flavor and texture, and a dollop of sherry bringing its own delightful quality.

The wine list is large but tends to be short on vintage information, and in a restaurant where wine prices can go above $50 a bottle, there is no excuse for not having all the facts available for the buyer.

Salads are first-rate, and desserts from the pastry cart are impressive.

JACK CARL'S TWO CENTS PLAIN
1114 Olive Street
436-1070

❖❖

Cuisine: Delicatessen, sandwiches
Serves: Lunch, Monday–Saturday
Prices: Moderate
Credit Cards: None
Dress: Casual
Reservations: Not applicable
Handicap Access: Satisfactory
Separate No-Smoking Section: No

Jack Carl serves lunch and laughter from behind the counter of the city's best Jewish delicatessen, and the sandwiches he creates have more staying power than the philosophy he dispenses, and far more flavor than the jokes he exchanges with a group of downtown businessmen who wait patiently in line.

Carl grew up in the delicatessen business; his father had a popular one in the University City Loop when I arrived in the area in 1955, and Jack had a busy one through the glory days of Gaslight Square. Memories remain in dozens of mementos that dot the walls.

Carl has top-quality standards in terms of corned beef, pastrami, brisket, chopped liver, and smoked tongue, with accoutrements like half-sour pickles, sour tomatoes, and knishes. He also offers a wide variety of salamis (Jewish, Italian, German) and tasty, if less exotic, foods like tuna, chicken, and egg salad.

All are served on fresh, tasty rolls and bread, and there's also an extensive inventory of beer and soda, all served while Carl's running commentary makes it almost fun to wait in line.

JOHN D. McGURK'S IRISH PUB
1200 Russell Blvd.
(Soulard area)
776-8309

‹›

Cuisine: Bar fare
Serves: Lunch and dinner, Monday–Saturday
Prices: Moderate
Credit Cards: All major
Dress: Casual
Reservations: Not applicable
Handicap Access: Satisfactory
Separate No-Smoking Section: No

The St. Louis version of the French cafe or the English pub—may the saints preserve us—is the mock-Irish bar, often called a pub but serving far better food than its English cousin. John D. McGurk's is one of many and is a pleasant place to visit for a snack or a sip. An exception can be made for the days bordering St. Patrick's Day, when a reprehensible St. Louis custom sometimes brings green dye to both beer and sawdust, improving the flavor of neither.

Over the last few years, McGurk's has expanded its seating area and its kitchen, and the meals have improved. Hamburgers and sandwiches are fine, soups are quite good and the Irish stew is usually excellent. Homemade potato chips, called Irish here, Welsh in other places, are crisp and tasty.

Service is brisk and there's a comfortable feel to McGurk's, though it can get noisy late at night, when Irish musicians often perform.

KEMOLL'S
211 North Broadway
Metropolitan Square Building
(Downtown)
421-0555

Cuisine: Italian
Serves: Dinner, every day; lunch, Monday–Friday
Prices: Expensive to very expensive
Credit Cards: All major
Dress: Informal
Reservations: Accepted, vital on weekends
Handicap Access: Satisfactory
Separate No-Smoking Section: Yes

For more than 60 years, Kemoll's Restaurant was a North St. Louis landmark. When residents of the area moved north and west, even when its best-known neighbors, the Cardinals, moved from Sportsman's Park to the downtown stadium in 1965, the Kemoll and Cusumano families remained.

Finally, downtown beckoned one more time, and the restaurant moved to new quarters in the impressively garish Metropolitan Square Building, lock, stock, and pasta pots.

The new Kemoll's seems slightly fussier in terms of service, but the menu is the same, with the old favorite specialties, and it's nice to report that the restaurant still is a family operation serving solid Italian food, freshly prepared and in large portions. It isn't merely a spaghetti house, either, but a white-tablecloth restaurant with an imaginative, talented kitchen.

Kemoll's prepares seafood appetizers in the Italian style as well as any restaurant in the city; clams Casino and steamed mussels are outstanding, and oysters on the half-shell are fresh, briny, and delicious. Fritti misti, a variety of lightly battered and quickly fried vegetables, long has been a signature dish, and calzone is splendid. Fresh, piping-hot cheese bread accompanies appetizers and is delicious. It's so good, in fact, that caution must be used so as not to ruin the appetite before the salad course, much less the entree.

Pastas, available as appetizers or entrees, are made on the premises, and they're special. Kemoll's is one of the handful of places in the city that serves real clams—whole ones and fresh chopped ones, in their own sauce—spoiling the diner for the canned variety. Fettuccine is delicious, and Kemoll's offers it with fresh tomatoes and prosciutto ham—a wonderful combination. Canneloni and tortellini are other pastas that are superior in any sauce.

There are steaks and a wide variety of simple and complex entrees. A traditional dish like veal Parmigiana is a delight, and a roast veal loin with a light, fresh tomato sauce is a winner, too. So is a giant veal chop.

Salads are excellent, vegetables are freshly cooked, and the wine list is long and quite complete—very strong on Italian varieties, with a good California selection too.

Desserts, also made on the premises, include rich, delicious cannoli and other Italian specialties, including a world-class crème brulée.

KENNEDY'S SECOND STREET COMPANY

612 North Second St.
(Laclede's Landing)

421-3655

Cuisine: Hamburgers, other bar fare
Serves: Lunch and dinner, every day; brunch on Sunday
Prices: Moderate
Credit Cards: All major
Dress: Casual
Reservations: Accepted
Handicap Access: Satisfactory
Separate No-Smoking Section: No

For almost a generation, there has been an effort to turn Laclede's Landing into a shopping and entertainment area, but little has happened. Steep cobblestone streets, limited parking, and unimaginative leadership have combined to keep the area unmemorable, with only a few bars and spots for musical entertainment showing success.

A lack of elegant restaurants has been another handicap. One of the pioneers in renovating the old and lovely warehouses of the neighborhood, Kennedy's combines a bar and dining area, with the charm of high ceilings, huge beams, and beautiful wood.

Like the other places in the Landing, Kennedy's doesn't offer great food, but prices are moderate and the sandwich-seafood-burger selection is satisfactory.

The noise level is high, but the fare is acceptable and the string quartet that often accompanies Sunday brunch is a nifty idea.

KEY WEST CAFE
Union Station
(Market Street, 18th to 20th Streets)
241-2566

Cuisine: Seafood, emphasizing shellfish
Serves: Lunch and dinner, every day
Prices: Moderate
Credit Cards: All major
Dress: Casual
Reservations: Not applicable
Handicap Access: Passable (narrow passage to rest rooms)
Separate No-Smoking Section: No

This casual, sometimes-raucous little place has fresh-ocean fish and shellfish, as well as conch chowder, as its Florida name would indicate. But the Key West specialties don't stop there. The best oyster stew in town comes out of this tiny kitchen, and when it comes to shucking fresh clams and delicious Blue Point oysters, the crew knows its business.

Conch, a very tough variety of giant snail, is hammered and ground for tenderizing, then made into first-rate chowder and fritters, with the latter benefiting from excellent batter and a heavy hand with the pepper. You can't hear the ocean, but they taste good.

The Key West is both bar and restaurant, and its location offers a good view of the passing parade at Union Station. A recent addition provides a slightly less noisy view.

Turtle soup is another winner, as are snack foods like shark and alligator bites, and the Cuban sandwich, similar to the New Orleans muffaletta, is large, sloppy, and delicious. The grouper sandwiches are first-rate, hamburgers are adequate, hot potato chips are excellent, and chili is ordinary.

For dessert, Key lime pie is marvelous, asserting the Key West as a generally superior downtown lunch spot.

LT. ROBERT E. LEE
100 South Leonor K. Sullivan Blvd.
241-1282

❖❖❖

Lt. Robert E. Lee closed in February 1992, but is scheduled to reopen in the summer under new management.

Cuisine: American
Serves: Lunch and dinner, every day; brunch on Sunday
Prices: Moderate to expensive
Credit Cards: All major
Dress: Informal
Reservations: Accepted, advised on weekends
Handicap Access: Difficult (cobblestones on levee, stairs to one of the dining rooms)
Separate No-Smoking Section: Yes

Long before he was a commanding general in the Confederate Army, Robert E. Lee was a lieutenant in the U.S. Army Corps of Engineers, working on flood control and navigation improvements on the Mississippi River. Hence the lower rank on this mock-antique riverboat that offers a lovely view of action on the river.

Located on the levee, the restaurant has three separate dining areas: a steak house, a seafood restaurant, and the Natchez Room, where there is often entertainment.

The decor is bright, and on sunny days it's a satisfactory place for lunch. In past visits, I've found the seafood room to offer superior meals to those in the other rooms, and many entrees, like the fish stew and some of the fresh seafood selections, are better than one would expect in a chain operation.

When Aunt Sally comes to town, it's a nice place to take her, and if she's brought the children, they'll like it too. The view is superior by day, when even big-city visitors will be mesmerized by the charm and the memory that the river can bring.

LUCIUS BOOMER
707 Clamorgan Alley
(Laclede's Landing)
621-8155

❖❖❖

Cuisine: Hamburgers, bar fare
Serves: Lunch and dinner, every day
Prices: Moderate
Credit Cards: MC, V
Dress: Casual
Reservations: Accepted
Handicap Access: Difficult (stairs)
Separate No-Smoking Section: No

This is another Laclede's Landing drink-and-eat spot, nicely decorated with photomurals showing the early days of the Eads Bridge and the Landing area. Owner John Clark, who has several similar operations in the area, decorates with flair and whimsy.

Like most of the neighborhood places, it's probably as much bar as restaurant, with a proper selection of generally satisfactory lunch items, good soups, and a better-than-average hamburger.

At night, the crowd is younger and the noise level becomes appreciably higher. Upstairs is another Clark operation, Jake's Steaks, featuring satisfactory steaks and all the trimmings.

McMURPHY'S GRILL
614 North 11th St.
231-3006

❖◦❖

Cuisine: American, with Irish overtones
Serves: Breakfast and lunch, Monday–Friday
Prices: Inexpensive
Credit Cards: None
Dress: Informal
Reservations: Not applicable
Handicap Access: Satisfactory
Separate No-Smoking Section: Yes

Eating well and doing good at the same time is a rare daily double, but McMurphy's Grill provides that opportunity.

The small downtown restaurant opened as a lunch spot and added breakfast about six months later. It is a work program to provide skills, experience, and jobs for people being helped by the St. Patrick Center, nearby. Grants from the McDonnell Douglas Foundation and the McDonnell Douglas Employees' Community Fund helped finance it, and the Pasta House Company provided restaurant expertise.

The result, in a building that had housed several restaurants in the past, is a bright, cheerful place with a limited lunch menu, but some delightful dishes, including tasty semi-Irish stew and outstanding meat loaf. "Semi-Irish" means that it is made with beef instead of lamb. Daily specials include such comfort foods as baked chicken with dressing, pork chops, chicken and dumplings, and braised short ribs.

Soups and sandwiches are pleasant, and breakfast choices include Irish soda bread, croissants, omelettes, and the like. Dessert choices are topped by a rich, delicious Bailey's Irish Cream cake—but doing good cuts the calories at least in half.

MIKE & MIN'S
925 Geyer St.
(Soulard area)
421-1655

Cuisine: American
Serves: Dinner, Tuesday–Saturday; lunch, Monday–Saturday
Prices: Moderate
Credit Cards: MC, V
Dress: Casual
Reservations: Accepted
Handicap Access: Entrance satisfactory, few steps to rest rooms
Separate No-Smoking Section: No

Long a Soulard area landmark, under several different ownerships, Mike & Min's has a gloriously carved antique back bar that is almost worth the trip, and a selection of imported beer and ale on draft that completes the reasons for visiting. At the same time, lunch is pleasant and the atmosphere nice. If it's Monday night, the Soulard Culture Squad may take over, providing space and time for neighborhood playwrights and poets.

The fare is generally standard, but the sandwiches are large enough to be more comfortably eaten with a knife and fork. A BLTA, or bacon, lettuce, tomato, and avocado is a good example, with the bacon thick and delicious and the whole-wheat toast showing nice texture. Another is the egg salad, tasty and heavy with mayonnaise, ready to erupt from the bread at a moment's notice.

Soups and hamburgers are standard, salads are good, and the aura is calm and relaxing.

MIKE SHANNON'S STEAKS AND SEAFOOD

100 North Seventh St.

421-1540

◆-◆

Cuisine: Steaks, seafood, and pasta
Serves: Dinner, every day; lunch, Monday–Friday
Prices: Expensive
Credit Cards: All major
Dress: Informal
Reservations: Accepted, advised on weekends
Handicap Access: Satisfactory
Separate No-Smoking Section: Yes

The name of the former Cardinal standout, now a radio announcer for the team, is emblazoned on the front door, but the establishment is operated by the Pasta House Company, which runs a large number of restaurants in the area. It's only a couple of blocks from Busch Stadium, and Shannon himself is a regular when the team is at home.

During baseball season, a Saturday night radio show with a sports theme originates here. The theme is extended with lots of photographs of Shannon adorning the walls, mingling with players in his playing days and bantering with broadcast types since he moved to the booth. Other sports memorabilia fills the empty spaces in the large, attractive restaurant.

Time was when anything but the most simple fare was risky, but there has been a large improvement in quality and variety since the first edition of this book.

Appetizers include fresh oysters and the St. Louis favorite, toasted ravioli, which supposedly was created in a local kitchen when someone tossed some raviolis into the deep fryer. Many people swear by them as an appetizer, but I find them generally tough and tasteless, wherever I eat them. Sliced onions, tomatoes, and mozzarella cheese are much better.

The Caesar salad is first-rate, and more successful to me than the Rich and Charlie's salad, named for the Pasta House founders and also for its very first restaurant. The salad is large, with well-chopped, fresh, crisp greens and dressing applied in liberal amounts. It's a local favorite, but I find it too heavy with dressing. I like salad dressing to heighten flavor but not replace it.

Steaks and chops remain the best bets, though there are some tasty Italian dishes too. Sirloins, filet mignon, and a giant 24-ounce porterhouse are usually excellent. Chicken breasts—broiled, blackened, or barbecued—are tasty, and so are pork chops.

The seafood selection has expanded, and there's a stylish touch along the way: the waiter brings a sheet with a dozen or so fish choices, then adds, "The ones with the prices are the ones we have." The system is sure and easy, and helps the diner. It's similar to one used by the Grand Central Oyster Bar, a high enough recommendation.

Vegetables and baked potatoes are satisfactory accompaniments.

The wine list is pleasing, with mostly California and a few French varieties. And as a change from the ubiquitous cheesecake, carrot cake is a splendid choice.

MISS HULLING'S CAFETERIA CATFISH & CRYSTAL RESTAURANT

Eleventh and Locust Streets
436-0840 (cafeteria), 231-7703 (restaurant)
Also: 8175 Big Bend Blvd.
(Webster Groves) 963-2200

❖❖❖

Cuisine: General American
Serves: Lunch and dinner, Monday–Saturday; breakfast in the cafeteria
Prices: Moderate
Credit Cards: All major
Dress: Informal
Reservations: Accepted in restaurant
Handicap Access: Satisfactory in all locations
Separate No-Smoking Section: Yes

Miss Hulling's Cafeteria has been a downtown landmark for half a century—a traditional cafeteria with traditional food. Catfish & Crystal, next door, serves the same menu, from the same kitchen, by friendly, competent personnel. White linen tops the tables, and drinks are available.

The Webster Groves location, which shares space with a retirement home, is just the same.

Florence Hulling became a St. Louis legend with her cakes and pies, fresh vegetables, and venerable Midwest dishes like chicken pot pie, beef stew, and fried catfish. Her son, Steve Apted, has carried on in similar style, and even if the cooking is not quite up to what it once was, it remains good, hearty, and filling, if sometimes bland.

The cafeteria is large, and the line reveals a glorious exhibit. All the bounties of the field are displayed, with dozens of vegetables and salads, and cakes and pies to tease even the slowest appetite. As in many cafeterias, it can be a test to measure if the eyes are larger than the stomach.

Next door, Catfish & Crystal occupies a room decorated with mementos and photos of old St. Louis. Like the cafeteria, it is not a gourmet restaurant, and like the cafeteria, the food is on the bland side, aimed at the slightly older clientele that the establishment attracts.

Soups and salads are outstanding, and the longtime standouts like Swiss steak, or chicken and dumplings, or roast pork are the best bets. Broiled fish is usually excellent too. Fried foods tend to be on the dry side, and sauces usually seem more like gravies. Vegetables are sometimes overcooked, but the southern tradition seems to encourage all vegetables to be overdone.

Breads and desserts are excellent, and there's a small wine list.

THE NINTH & RUSSELL RESTAURANT

2028 South Ninth St.
(corner of Russell Blvd.)

773-5565

❖━━━━━━━━━━━━━━━━━━━━━━━━━━━━━━━━━━❖

Cuisine: American bar food
Serves: Lunch and dinner, every day
Prices: Inexpensive to moderate
Credit Cards: All major
Dress: Casual
Reservations: Not applicable
Handicap access: Satisfactory
Separate No-Smoking Area: No

The large collection of bourbon bottles behind the bar is evidence of a place that understands history, maybe even remembers the time when a neighborhood saloon, like this one, had brands for everyone.

The Ninth & Russell, taking its name from the address in the Soulard neighborhood, has a comforting stateliness and decor reminiscent of an English pub.

The menu, good for both lunch and dinner, goes in an opposite direction, with a full string of barbecue specialties including smoked beef brisket and pork butt, pork steaks, and ribs. Both brisket and butt were exemplary—tender, richly flavored, and good enough to stand on their own without sauce.

Hamburgers are outstanding, and the house special potatoes are splendid—red potato chunks sautéd with butter, parsley, and lots of garlic. Some chunks are crisp on the edges; all are hot and tasty.

Desserts are pleasant, like everything else at The Ninth & Russell.

43

O. T. HODGE CHILE– OR CHILI–PARLOR

Union Station (Downtown) **421-9938**

611 Pine St. (Downtown) **436-3136**

9705 Watson Rd. (Mid-County) **966-5151**

3523 N. Broadway (Downtown) **342-9562**

1620 S. Jefferson Ave. (Downtown) **772-1215**

4060 Chouteau Ave. (Downtown) **533-9677**

Cuisine: Chili and variations
Serves: Union Station, 24 hours; others: breakfast, lunch and dinner, most weekdays. Phone for specifics.
Prices: Inexpensive
Credit Cards: No
Dress: Casual
Reservations: Not applicable.
Handicap Access: Passable
Separate No-Smoking Section: No

Whether it's chili or chile, and whether run by an original Hodge or not, this group of restaurants offers standard chili, with or without beans and tamales. Each one features that crucial St. Louis breakfast legend, the "slinger," or fried eggs with chili.

The original O. T. Hodge's was at 812 Pine Street, a location that made way for a modern telecommunications building. It was a legend for steaming, greasy chili in old white-china bowls and for the neighborhood clientele who patronized it in the early-morning hours and often slept in the doorway afterward.

Times have changed. There's an outlet in Union Station that is handy for the wee hours; some of the others look much like the original, while some even have greenery and ferns for the lunch crowd.

The chili is pretty good, if not as greasy as it once was. The beef is ground rather than chopped, but that seems to have become the norm these days, and more's the pity.

Chili for lunch is all right, but I prefer it as the final stop of a long evening of eating and drinking, when the body needs some extra fire to make it home to bed.

PARK AVENUE CAFE
1923 Park Ave.
241-9122

Cuisine: Modern American
Serves: Dinner, Wednesday–Saturday; Lunch, Monday–Friday
Prices: Expensive
Credit Cards: All major
Dress: Informal
Reservations: Accepted for large parties
Handicap Access: Entrance satisfactory, rest room impossible (stairs)
Separate No-Smoking Section: Yes

When Richard Cole opened the Park Avenue Cafe, he was stepping into queen-sized shoes. The charming storefront in the Lafayette Square neighborhood had been home to the Cafe Zoe, and earlier to the Empire Cafe, two places that gave new meaning to lunch in the downtown area.

It took Cole a little while, but he now has found his own voice in the kitchen, and his operation adds the same elegance—with different flavors—to lunch and to dinner.

The cuisine is modern American with California touches. Presentation is lovely, and there is much use of fresh vegetables, sometimes grilled, sometimes marinated and served raw. Those who like a big chef's salad for lunch will find a touch of heaven here.

Grilled shrimp, first marinated with garlic and basil, make a superior appetizer, and so does the crab puff, a light, delightful puff pastry filled with crabmeat. Barbecued oysters are less satisfactory, with the sauce too hot and strong for the oysters. The same sauce, however, works well on a toasted crabmeat sandwich for lunch. A combination of rolled Brie and chevre cheeses with smoked salmon is pretty, but the cheese tends to overpower the delicate flavor of the salmon.

Salmon, nicely grilled and served with cilantro butter, is a treat, and charred tuna, still rare in the middle, shows superior flavor and texture.

A flank steak sandwich that is a lunch special is perked up with hints of ginger and a superior marinade, and dinner choices also include lamb chops and a filet mignon, plus a couple of chicken breasts with different sauces.

The dessert tray displays a rich, not-too-sweet carrot cake, and one day offered a banana cheesecake that was unusual and spectacular. Service is smooth and highly professional, and the wine list is better than average.

PREMIO
701 Market Street
231-0911

Cuisine: Italian
Serves: Dinner, Monday–Saturday; lunch, Monday–Friday
Prices: Expensive to very expensive
Credit Cards: All major
Dress: Informal (jackets preferred for men)
Reservations: Accepted
Handicap Access: Satisfactory
Separate No-Smoking Section: No

The room is brighter and the cuisine lighter, and it's open for lunch, but in all other respects, Premio is every bit as splendid an Italian restaurant as owner Dominic Galati's original Hill location, Dominic's.

Located in the heart of downtown, Premio is not just another Dominic's. The menu is smaller, the sauces a little lighter, and more dishes are grilled or broiled than fried or sautéd. There's olive oil on the table, a delightful, flavorful substitute for butter. It's a little messier, but it tastes great, and someone told me that it's better for you, too, though I'd never let something like that cloud my judgment.

There are a number of pasta entrees, plus a fish of the day, veal in the sauce of the day, a half-rack of lamb, and several other standards.

Roasted peppers, redolent of olive oil and improved by a couple of anchovies, are a marvelous appetizer, and the red and green peppers, on a plate dotted with fresh mozzarella cheese, looks a bit like the Italian flag. Carpaccio is right, with just a touch of cheese and not enough to kill the delicate beef flavor. Fried calamari in a light, crisp batter, was tender and flavorful, and steamed mussels, in white wine, lemon, and garlic, were plump and juicy.

Papardelle, a thin, wide noodle, is enriched with a duck sauce that shows off the delicate flavor of the fowl, and ravioli stuffed with ricotta cheese is a rich combination of tastes. Linguine with seafood sauce is another treat.

Grilled beef tenderloin with a sauce of marrow and wild mushrooms is simple, but the flavors complement one another perfectly, and traditional veal in Marsala sauce was perfectly balanced.

The wine list is splendid, strong on good Italian labels and solid California selections, but it's on the high side. Service is as poised and elegant as it is at the Hill location, and cassata cake and cannoli, both impressive, lead the dessert choices.

RUTH'S CHRIS STEAK HOUSE
Eleventh and Walnut Streets
241-7711

❖•❖

Cuisine: Steaks and chops
Serves: Dinner, every day
Prices: Very expensive
Credit Cards: All major
Dress: Informal
Reservations: Accepted
Handicap Access: Satisfactory (elevator from lobby to dining room)
Separate No-Smoking Section: Yes

Despite the efforts of the food freaks, there are people—healthy people—who still emphatically endorse the idea of properly cooked good beef, and there are steak houses like Ruth's Chris that remain to serve them.

Ruth's Chris is a chain operation based in New Orleans, and it offers lovely beef and huge lobsters. The restaurant is handsome, with dark wood, crisp tablecloths, and gleaming silver and crystal. The menu is simple, with steaks, chops, a few broiled fish selections, and lobsters that live in a tank until a diner orders one, at which time it is captured, weighed, and sold by the pound.

Everything is à la carte, and portions are huge; the waiter recommended one vegetable or potato for two people, and it was an excellent suggestion. Steaks are uniformly excellent—juicy, tender, and cooked just the way they're ordered. They are broiled in lots of butter, which adds additional flavor and cholesterol, but they can be cooked without it if you prefer.

Sirloin, rib eye, and filet mignon all were outstanding, and the really hungry group can order porterhouses in sizes for two, three, or four people. The lobsters range from two to five pounds, or so says the menu. Giant lobsters are impressive on the plate, but I've usually found them on the tough side, so I asked for a small one, got one at just over two pounds, and loved every bite of it.

Appetizers show the restaurant's New Orleans background, with items like barbecued shrimp, shrimp in remoulade sauce, and Cajun popcorn (fried crayfish) in addition to stuffed mushrooms, fried onion rings, and fried squid.

One appetizer will suffice for two people, two are plenty for three diners, and we ordered one appetizer and one salad, giving both of us a sufficiency. The remoulade sauce is excellent, but both the crayfish and the squid had little flavor. The standard house salad is good, but the menu shows several others, including a huge, chilled, crisp chunk of iceberg lettuce, a salad I happen to like with steak. The Thousand Island dressing was tangy and tasty, and while I know plain iceberg lettuce is scorned in some circles, there are times when it is just right.

Potatoes (also à la carte) are available in a wide range of preparation. Foil-wrapped baked potatoes can be discounted on sight, as far as I'm concerned. Chips were excellent, sliced very thin and fried very crisp, then drained so as to be extremely dry. They do tend to cool off rapidly, which the waiter advised in regretful tones, but they were delicious. Lyonnaise potatoes were tasty but could have been hotter.

The wine list is solid, and given the fare, the desire usually is for hearty reds, like California cabernet sauvignons or French bordeaux.

Desserts bring an afterglow of even more rich food, though fresh fruit is available, and a pecan cheesecake was outstanding. Bread pudding was passable but very strong in alcohol flavor, with an uninteresting sauce.

SIDNEY STREET CAFE
2000 Sidney St.
(Soulard area)
771-5777

Cuisine: Modern American
Serves: Dinner, Tuesday–Saturday; lunch, Tuesday–Friday
Prices: Moderate to expensive
Credit Cards: All major
Dress: Informal
Reservations: Accepted (recommended on weekends)
Handicap Access: Satisfactory
Separate No-Smoking Section: Yes

Defining "American cuisine" these days is like defining an "American person." Each have had so much influence, both hereditary and environmental, that it's almost impossible to set down rules that would provide proper identification.

The Sidney Street Cafe, a comfortable, pleasant place to dine, serves what I call "American cuisine," but it reveals influences of all types, some still showing their birthplace with a hyphen, others already blended into complete Americanism.

Sidney Street is a warm and relaxing spot, with an attractive, paneled dining room and highly professional service. In the kitchen, there is considerable imagination and a calm, knowing hand with herbs and spices. The chalkboard menu changes with the seasons, and both appetizers and entrees have been winners.

The appetizer list can be truly cross-cultural, with such items as French onion soup, Mexican tostadas, Oriental spring rolls, Eastern European strudel, and Italian pasta. Better than any, however, is a blue cheese tart that is tangy, light, and wonderful. Stuffed mushrooms are excellent, and French onion soup is good, though the bowl is stuffed with so much onion, bread, and cheese that there's hardly any room for the liquid.

Lamb chops with a honey-mustard glaze are a treat, and pasta with seafood sauce also scores high. Poached salmon is cooked to the perfect moment, then topped with a light hollandaise sauce. Grilled chicken with a raspberry sauce is a delight, with the chicken moist and tender, and the tart berries a perfect complementary flavor.

Grilled tuna steak, charred on the outside, rosy pink in the middle, is superior, and tortellini stuffed with gorgonzola cheese is both unusual and delicious.

The wine list is small but sufficient. And the desserts are heavily chocolate, like a double-rich brownie with ice cream and chocolate sauce. There are other choices, however, like a spectacular apple crumb pie, nicely flavored with cinnamon.

THE STATION GRILLE
Hyatt Regency Hotel
Union Station, Market Street
(18th to 20th Sts.)
231-1234

Cuisine: Seafood, grilled steaks
Serves: Dinner Monday–Saturday, brunch on Sunday
Prices: Very expensive
Credit Cards: All major
Dress: Informal (jackets preferred)
Reservations: Accepted
Handicap Access: Satisfactory (if elevator is available)
Separate No-Smoking Section: Yes

First an Omni, now a Hyatt. First the American Rotisserie, then the Sea Grill, now the Station Grille.

Under any ownership, management, or chef, this has remained one of the most beautiful dining rooms in the city, with high ceilings and light wood paneling contrasting with brass fixtures. Well-placed banquettes offer a feeling of privacy, and the open grill at the west end, with fowl turning slowly, is a lovely touch.

While the room has been a beautiful constant ever since the hotel opened as a flagship of the rehabbed Union Station, the restaurant itself has been more variable, and less successful.

The emphasis remains on broiled or grilled meats and fish, but the selection is smaller than it once was, and the preparation doesn't show the same imagination, although service has remained strong through the years.

Spicing shows southwestern overtones, and there are some excellent ideas on the menu, but at the Station Grille's prices, which allow little margin for error, execution too often falls short.

Roasted garlic soup was a brilliant dish, with a layer of cream on top adding a lovely touch to the flavor of the garlic, lightened to a pleasant tang by cooking. Lobster bisque, in contrast, was most ordinary, and the few pieces of lobster were tough.

Interestingly, fish selections were much less appealing than meat, with lamb and chicken perfectly grilled, while seafood tended to be overcooked. Vegetables are variable.

Desserts, from a handsome trolley, were good, and the wine list, though on the expensive side, has some superior bottles.

The Station Grille looks like a great restaurant, and on occasion it has come close. On other occasions, it has been far away. A real commitment to excellence and more consistency from the kitchen would help.

THE TAP ROOM AT THE ST. LOUIS BREWERY

2100 Locust Street
(entrance on 21st Street between Olive and Locust Streets)
241-2337

Cuisine: American and English pub grub
Serves: Lunch and dinner, Monday–Saturday
Prices: Inexpensive to moderate
Credit Cards: All major
Dress: Casual
Reservations: Not applicable
Handicap Access: Difficult (steps at front door)
Separate No-Smoking Section: Yes

The city's first brew-pub arrived with 1992, marking the first new brewery in the city in at least a half-century and, it is hoped, another beacon to bring people to the downtown area.

Considering its German heritage—and its beer heritage—this late arrival to a growing national trend may be a surprise, but the very presence of giant Anheuser-Busch may have had a depressing effect through the years. Brew-pubs came to other states, and finally, on-site brewing and selling of beer cleared the state legislature in 1990. Anheuser-Busch did not object and did not even send its lobbyist to the hearings, but then again, Anheuser-Busch probably spills more beer in one morning than this small-time St. Louis Brewery will make in a year.

The Tap Room, with high ceilings, gigantic beams and lots of light, is in a building that once housed a printer, and the brewing process takes place on one side, behind huge windows. Watching beer brew is a little more exciting than watching grass grow, but there are those who like it.

Beer and ale are served on draught from behind a long, steel-topped bar, with only on-premises consumption allowed. Beer is served in generous, English-style sizes, in pints and half-pints. The English pint, however, holds 20 ounces.

The Tap Room began with three ales and a stout and will be changing styles as time goes on. A pilsner was scheduled to be the next release.

The brews are rich, hearty, and excellent, and so is the food. The hamburger is served on an English muffin, the delicious, smoky bratwurst is accompanied by cinnamon-tangy, homemade applesauce, and there's classic blackstrap rye for the liverwurst and onion sandwich.

Smoked turkey and grilled chicken breast are other sandwiches, and there are salads and some fruit, cheese, and smoked meat plates. Fish and chips are a highlight, with the french fries (that's what the English call chips) crisp and hot and delicious, served with a fiery ketchup and a tangy mayonnaise sauce on the side.

Sticky toffee pudding, an English-style cake with dates and other goodies, is dense and horrendously rich, thanks to lots of caramel sauce and real whipped cream.

As the Racing Form would say, "Fast out of the gate, with bloodlines to go the distance."

TONY'S
10 South Broadway
231-7007

❖❖

Cuisine: Italian
Serves: Dinner, Monday–Saturday
Prices: Very expensive
Credit Cards: All major
Dress: Jackets required for men
Reservations: Accepted
Handicap Access: Satisfactory
Separate No-Smoking Section: No

Every city has its premier restaurant—the dining establishment against which all others are measured. In St. Louis, Tony's holds that position, and has held it for more than 30 years. Challengers come and go, many of them having learned the business at Tony's, but as good as some of them are, all they have achieved is to make Vince Bommarito work harder to maintain his primacy.

A new challenge faces Bommarito in 1992; Tony's is in the path of construction of a new football stadium and expansion of the convention center. As a result, the restaurant will move nine blocks south, to the site of Anthony's, opened by Vince and his brother, Anthony, in 1972 and closed in 1990. It also will utilize some of the space where Brooks Brothers stood before its move, providing the same number of seats, but on a single level.

Elegant and polished, with exceptional food and service, Tony's has won the Holiday Magazine Award every year it has been given, and perennially earns five stars from Mobil.

Vince and Tony Bommarito got into the restaurant business when their father died. He had run a small, checked-tablecloth spaghetti joint, across the street from the bus station. Vince, the elder, dreamed of a great, elegant restaurant, something the city sorely needed at the time, and the two young men soon achieved it.

Until 1972, they labored there together, Vince usually out front, Tony usually in the kitchen. When they built Anthony's, Tony moved there and Vince remained at Tony's. Since Anthony's closed, Tony Bommarito has become a wholesale wine merchant.

Today, Vince's son, Vince Jr., is a key member of the staff at Tony's, working both in the kitchen and on the floor, where he looks to be a chip off the old block. A spectacular crême brulée, and a magnificent risotto with gorgonzola cheese, are just a couple of his contributions. He's an alumnus of the Culinary Institute of America, and while the proud father won't come right out and say so, it's obvious that he thinks the restaurant will be in good hands for another generation.

As a restaurateur, Bommarito is a classic host. He checks the room continually, stops at every table, introduces himself to unfamiliar customers, and visits with old friends. At the same time, he is making sure that everything is perfect; not even the smallest smudge on a water glass misses his seemingly casual eye.

Bommarito takes orders, suggests dishes, helps serve, and is a constant presence. For many years, he almost never missed a night when the restaurant was open. I was there one evening when he was in the hospital, in the recovery room after shoulder surgery and still checking in every hour or so, still recommending dishes to regular customers.

In his own way, he has also provided a training academy— many of the city's better Italian restaurants are owned by men who worked as waiters at Tony's, and he enjoys the challenge. It tickles him to be first in town with a menu item, like a huge veal chop, and then to see his "students" adopt it.

Like most restaurateurs, Bommarito loves the experimental diner; he truly enjoys recommending something different and then seeing it devoured with pleasure. When taking an order, he may suggest against successive courses that are too similar, and he is quick to remind diners of their favorite dishes.

I admire the myriad of small things that makes the dining

experience at Tony's so special. When you have a leftover wrapped, for example, you don't carry it out of the restaurant; you find it waiting in the car. And you don't get a car check, but when you stroll out of the restaurant after dinner, it seems to arrive automatically. The same magic takes place in the coat check room, and so have some wonderful romantic gestures, like the woman who checked a cloth coat and received a mink, a birthday surprise from her husband, who had stashed it there earlier in the day.

At the same time, I sometimes am irritated by the tendency to hover that some waiters show; I don't like it when I am lighting a match, only to have an eager waiter practically leap between it and my cigarette with his own light.

And the food?

Over the years, Tony's sauces have become lighter, and there's a lot more seafood on the menu than there was. Pastas are made on the premises, and many herbs are grown here, too. But veal Parmigiana, Marsala, and Piccatta remain—and remain favorites.

Lobster albanello, which Bommarito says is the most ordered dish, has been on the menu as long as I can remember, and I ate my first meal at Tony's in 1956. The lobster dish involves large chunks of real lobster in a rich wine-and-cream sauce.

Steaks, chops, beautiful lamb, massive veal, and a wide variety of fresh fish are available, all beautifully cooked and served with style and imagination.

There's something about fresh clams in pasta with clam sauce that will spoil you forever for the canned ones. Pasta can be eaten as appetizer, main course, or side dish. Bommarito's favorite pasta, by the way, is rigatoni, a large, ribbed noodle that he says absorbs sauce better than the extra-thin varieties people often order.

Truffles and wild mushrooms are used in many dishes, and the creamed spinach is the best I know. Italian potatoes—sliced thin, sautéd in olive oil with onions and black olives, and crisped on the edges—are simply spectacular.

Roasted peppers, chopped eggplant relish, mussels in garlic-flavored broth, and carpaccio all make excellent appetizers. And

60

there are pâtés, snails, steak tartar, and caviar for those who think French.

The wine list is lengthy and superior, with bottles to match any taste or budget. Desserts are also made on the premises, and the pastries are rich and wonderful. Cassata cake can be very special, as is tiramisu, which shows up less frequently, and there's always fruit and cheese, plus an impressive zabaglione. Young Vince's crême brulée matches any served anywhere.

When everything's right—and it almost always is—Tony's provides the ultimate dining experience and undoubtedly will continue to do so in its new location.

TOP OF THE RIVERFRONT
Clarion Hotel
200 South 4th St.
241-3191

Cuisine: American
Serves: Dinner, every day; lunch, Monday–Friday; Sunday brunch
Prices: Moderate to expensive
Credit Cards: All major
Dress: Informal
Reservations: Accepted
Handicap Access: Entrance satisfactory, rest rooms difficult (stairs)
Separate No-Smoking Section: Yes

The best place to dine and see the city at the same time is at the revolving top of this urban hotel tower, where the riverfront and downtown sparkle or glow, depending on the time of day. For a number of years, only the view was worth recommending, but things have changed for the better, and now the excuse of out-of-town visitors is not always necessary.

After all, the city looks nice to its own residents, too.

The menu is general American, with some good grilled dishes, accompanied by standard appetizers and desserts. Service is both friendly and competent.

TUCKER'S PLACE
2117 South 12th St.
(Soulard area)
772-5977

Cuisine: American, primarily steaks
Serves: Dinner, Tuesday–Sunday; lunch, Tuesday–Friday
Prices: Moderate
Credit Cards: MC, V
Dress: Casual
Reservations: Not accepted
Handicap Access: A few steps for entrance, rest rooms difficult
Separate No-Smoking Section: No

There's top sirloin or filet mignon, and there's filet mignon or top sirloin—with two sizes of the filet. Time was when that was the choice at Tucker's Place, and that's still the primary choice for diners seeking uncommon value, perhaps tops in the city. This small restaurant-bar in Soulard has built a citywide reputation on beef and its traditional accessories, properly cooked and served.

Steaks arrive tender, tasty, and prepared as ordered, and a baked potato, on my last visit, was outstanding, with lengthy cooking bringing the inside to a lovely mealy texture while the skin was nicely charred. Best of all, there was no foil in evidence.

Hamburgers and roast beef sandwiches also are available, along with the ubiquitous pizza, a few appetizers, soups, and salads. Onion soup was delightful, and so were dinner salads, standard in terms of greens, but fresh and crisp, with pleasant dressings.

There's house wine from a carafe, and it's passable, and so are desserts.

At Tucker's Place, however, the steak's the thing, and it's a winner.

CENTRAL WEST END
(Plus Pershing-DeBaliviere)

Including Midtown and Pershing-DeBaliviere

Balaban's
Bar Italia
C. Whittaker's American Bistro
Cafe Alexander (Pershing-DeBaliviere)
Culpeppers
Dressel's
Duff's
Grappa
Kopperman's
Llywelyn ap Gruffyd
Museum Cafe (Art Museum, Forest Park)
Nantucket Cove
Redel's (Pershing-DeBaliviere)
Sansui
Shalimar Garden
Sunshine Inn
Tom's Bar & Grill

BALABAN'S
405 North Euclid Ave.
361-8085

◆-◆

Cuisine: American-French
Serves: Lunch and dinner, every day; brunch, Saturday–Sunday
Prices: Expensive
Credit Cards: All major
Dress: Informal
Reservations: Until 6:30 p.m. or for large parties
Handicap Access: Satisfactory, but getting through bar area can sometimes be difficult
Separate No-Smoking Section: Yes

When longtime employees Tom Flynn, Steve McIntyre, and Bryan Young bought Balaban's from Herb and Adelaide Balaban, St. Louis fans of this bright light of informal, delightful dining in the city's Central West End held their collective breaths.

Not to worry.

Balaban's has retained the charm of its eclectic and individualistic character and has risen to new culinary heights.

When Balaban opened the restaurant in 1972, helping to change the face of St. Louis dining, it had a rather casual-hippy atmosphere, though it always boasted white tablecloths and crisp linen. Waiters were informal and so was the decor, highlighted by glorious French theatrical posters. It was probably Herb himself—wandering around in T-shirts, jeans, and suspenders—who set the style.

The new triumvirate has a similar outlook but has expanded the menu and reached far and wide for the very best raw materials. Oysters from far-flung coastal areas are regular items, and the cooking style has stretched to include herbs and spices from the

Southwest, fruit from the Caribbean, and taste sensations that sometimes seem heaven-sent.

At the same time, old and classic favorites like chilled cucumber soup, beef Wellington, and rack of lamb have remained vital parts of the kitchen's repertoire.

The nouvelle fad came and went, but sauces remained on the lighter side, as did the emphasis on seafood. Fresh seasonal fare meant shad roe from the Hudson River and soft shell crabs from Chesapeake Bay. The shell crabs are as well prepared as any I've tasted. Crab cakes, however, suffer from too much filling.

A veal chop stuffed with shiitake mushrooms and fresh salmon grilled and served in a flavorful, light-hearted black bean sauce were highlights of recent visits.

Balaban's also boasts one of the finest wine lists in the city, with intelligent pricing and superior selection of both imported and domestic varieties.

Desserts are as elegant as everything that has gone before, including home-made ice creams to accompany superb fruit tarts.

Balaban's remains a place to see or be seen. It's a series of rooms, beginning with a roofed and windowed sidewalk cafe where lunch is served and the people-watching is a highlight, especially in the summer. Moving inside at dinner brings one to a bar area where the noise level ranges from uncomfortable to unbearable. Having survived that rite of passage, however, the dining rooms are generally calm and quiet—and the dining experience is a superior one.

BAR ITALIA
4656 Maryland Ave.
361-7010

❖❖

Cuisine: Italian
Serves: Lunch and dinner, Tuesday–Sunday
Prices: Moderate to expensive
Credit Cards: AE, MC, V
Dress: Casual
Reservations: Not accepted
Handicap Access: Entrance satisfactory, rest room difficult
Separate No-Smoking Section: Yes

Mengesha Yohannes came from Eritrea to St. Louis to study medicine. To earn some extra money, he began working at Bar Italia, the best and most authentic Italian cafe in town. Today, his medical studies ended, Yohannes owns Bar Italia, and it still is the best and most authentic Italian cafe in the city.

Bar Italia began as a coffee and dessert house in the Central West End, with all the pastries from authentic recipes, most of them hand carried from the Old Country. Expansion brought a lunch and dinner menu, but the authenticity never changed. Neither did the casual atmosphere that makes this a wonderful stop for newspaper reading and coffee sipping in the midafternoon.

Turn away from the traffic, and you'll think you are in Italy or France.

The menu is usually the same throughout the day, though there may be a special or two prepared in time for dinner. Caprini and crostini lead the appetizer list, the former a large chunk of fresh goat cheese marinated in olive oil and chili peppers, served with bread and olives. The latter, described as "the original Italian version of what the French call canapes," consists of toasted slices of crusty bread topped with a little pâté, or an olive spread, or cheese.

Both are splendid, as is carpaccio, or paper-thin slices of raw beef with a little olive oil drizzled on top and a handful of capers. Too many local restaurants kill the flavor of the beef with too much oil or cheese, but Bar Italia uses a light hand and serves hard Parmesan cheese on the side. Perfect.

Caponata, a relish that is primarily chopped eggplant but also includes roasted peppers, olives, and lots of garlic, is another winner. A roasted pepper appetizer is delightful, and fresh, plump, juicy mussels in white wine and their own liquid or in a light, tomato-based sauce, are superior as either appetizer or entree.

Entrees include several pasta dishes, plus a few fish, chicken, and veal selections—all fresh and delightful, with a lovely piquancy to many sauces. Pasta with sausage and chicken, or with shrimp, calamari, and mussels are my favorites. Another outstanding choice is the vitello tonato, or poached veal served at room temperature with a tuna, caper, and olive oil sauce.

Chicken with a Venetian-style sauce of vinegar, raisins, pine nuts, and mint is yet another example of the imagination in the Bar Italia kitchen.

The wine list includes a good selection of Italian varieties, and there also are Italian aperitifs, digestifs, grappas, and soft drinks.

Room must be saved for dessert, and it's proper to walk inside the restaurant and press your nose against the display case. There are flourless cakes, rich pastries, tortes, and tarts, and spectacular home-made gelati and sorbets. As accompaniments, there are a wide variety of elegant chocolate and coffee drinks, served hot or cold, and with or without whipped cream.

Dollar for dollar, Bar Italia is one of the best restaurant values in the city, and Yohannes one of the most charming hosts.

C. WHITTAKER'S AMERICAN BISTRO
236 North Euclid Ave.
361-7771

‣‣

Cuisine: Modern American-Italian
Serves: Lunch and dinner every day, brunch on Sunday
Prices: Moderate to expensive
Credit Cards: All major
Dress: Informal
Reservations: Accepted
Handicap Access: Passable (room can be crowded)
Separate No-Smoking Section: Yes

Cecil Whittaker is an odd name for a pizzeria, especially in a city with as strong an Italian heritage as this one. But the name worked, and the pizzerias have been successful. Now, with an updated black-and-white decor and a Central West End location, we have C. Whittaker's American Bistro, a newcomer in late 1991.

The space once was Zimfel's, a restaurant, bar, and wine store, and Wendy Zimet, a partner in that operation, is running the old shop with new decor.

The main menu has lots of pizza, pasta, salad, sandwich, and appetizer selections, good for lunch as well as dinner. There also are four specials, one each beginning with beef, veal, chicken, and fish.

A single visit I made early in its career was highly satisfactory. The fast pace, crowded room, and slightly noisy atmosphere all conspire to make people feel they're having fun and are part of a "scene."

Escargots—in a traditional sauce, on a bed of puff pastry, but accented with chunks of roquefort cheese—were excellent. Green-lipped New Zealand mussels in a mustard sauce were also tasty, but on the tough side.

70

Risotto, which gained a lot of ground on St. Louis menus in the early '90s, was tasty, though the rice had not absorbed all the sauce. Mushrooms helped, and a grilled chicken breast on top was juicy and splendid. The beef special, tournedos in an outstanding bordelaise sauce, featured delicious fork-tender beef on a very busy plate with hot zucchini, spinach, mushrooms, and cold tomatoes and onions.

A side dish of pasta in marinara sauce showed a cultivated, careful preparation: a sufficient amount of garlic with good spicing and olives over pasta that was properly al dente.

The wine list is a nice one, but the restaurant has the unfortunate habit of adding tax to the bottle without indicating such a policy, meaning that $20 on the list will be about $21.60 on the check.

Homemade tiramisu was outstanding, rich and creamy and properly soaked with alcohol.

C. Whittaker's is a newcomer with promise.

CAFE ALEXANDER
5513 Pershing Ave.
367-7755

Cuisine: Russian-American
Serves: Dinner, Tuesday–Saturday
Prices: Moderate to expensive
Credit Cards: MC, V
Dress: Casual
Reservations: Accepted
Handicap Access: Satisfactory
Separate No-Smoking Section: No

From a warm storefront location in the city's Pershing-De-Baliviere neighborhood. St. Louis's only Russian restaurant serves up memories of my boyhood. My grandmother, like the owners of the Cafe Alexander, was a Russian emigre, and she prepared many of the same dishes.

The three B's of Russian cuisine—borscht, blintzes, and blinis—all are excellent. The borscht sings, whether it's of cabbage or beet origin. I prefer both to schav, the so-called "spinach borscht," usually a summer dish served well chilled.

Blintzes are crêpes, rolled around many different fillings. They're usually a sweet dish, stuffed with cheese and topped with sugar, cinnamon, sour cream, and fruit. Blini are extremely thin buckwheat pancakes, often topped with caviar. In a perfect world, the caviar would always be big black beluga from giant sturgeons, but one can still savor the way they are served here—with good-quality red salmon caviar and rich sour cream.

Eggplant dip can be found in Italian, Middle Eastern, Greek, and other ethnic restaurants, but Cafe Alexander's is outstanding, with plenty of garlic in a coarse blend of superior flavor. Pelmenyi, like a giant ravioli filled with chicken, is very tasty.

The house specialty is "booterbrot," a giant sandwich. Well, almost a sandwich. It's a large pile of meat, cheese, and lettuce, wrapped and baked in a pastry crust. The crust is similar to that of a beef Wellington, the inside has overtones of a Reuben, or a poor boy, or even a gyro, and it's tasty and filling. Knife and fork are necessary.

Stews and goulash have been satisfactory, if not outstanding. Desserts are rich and pleasant. Service can be erratic, but it's always friendly, and I'm sorry Cafe Alexander stopped serving breakfast because it was outstanding, and the fried potatoes were memorable.

CULPEPPERS

300 North Euclid Ave.
(Central West End) **361-2828**

12316 Olive Blvd. (West) **469-3888**

❖◦❖

Cuisine: American
Serves: Lunch and dinner, every day
Prices: Inexpensive to moderate
Credit Cards: MC, V
Dress: Casual
Reservations: Not accepted
Handicap Access: Satisfactory
Separate No-Smoking Section: No

After a brilliant decade in the Central West End, Culpeppers was sold, and the new owners opened a second spot in the West County. Thankfully, the splendid sandwiches and soups that had made the original a personal favorite did not change much, and the new location used old recipes to satisfy new audiences.

More bar than restaurant, the original Culpeppers brought miracles from a tiny kitchen, and the summer specials of ceviche and gazpacho were memorable. The former, made of baby scallops, marinated in lime juice and a few spices, then tossed with bits of avocado, is one of the finest appetizers I know. Gazpacho is also delicious, but so are all the soups, from beef barley to clam chowder to oxtail to cream of artichoke to my favorite, peppery hot Italian sausage.

There's chili too, but it's pretty ordinary, and no match for the soups.

Culps (as we tend to call it) introduced so-called Buffalo chicken wings to the city and still serves them with the proper tang. The sandwich menu includes a monster bacon, lettuce, and tomato, superior club and spicy barbecued pork steak, as well as hamburgers and hot dogs. Pastrami and some "melts" are available, but they don't measure up to the other sandwiches.

The new owners added a satisfactory chicken salad but made minimal other adjustments.

In addition to providing superior sandwiches, Culpeppers is a first-class bar that caters to adults. A sign in the window indicates that children under 12 are not welcome. As for me, I've always felt that no-children sections were more necessary in restaurants and bars than no-smoking sections.

DRESSEL'S
419 North Euclid Ave.
361-1060

❖-❖

Cuisine: Welsh pub grub with American overtones
Serves: Lunch and dinner, every day
Prices: Inexpensive to moderate
Credit Cards: MC, V
Dress: Casual
Reservations: Not accepted
Handicap Access: Satisfactory
Separate No-Smoking Section: No

It would be pretentious to call Dressel's Pub a literary hangout, but there are many St. Louis writers and musicians who spend time at this warm, charming Central West End bar-restaurant. Owner Jon Dressel is a poet, and iambic is spoken here.

Pictures of composers, poets, and writers line the walls, and the influence of musicians is reflected in the collection of tapes the bartender brings forth. The bar is a long, narrow oval, and tables line the walls around it.

Service is brisk and very efficient, and the menu points out that servers don't have particular stations but help out as needed. The system works, too.

Recently, the owners turned an upstairs room into "The Pub Above" —as close a re-creation to an English pub as I've seen in this country. It's warm and cozy, serves drinks, desserts, and a few snacks, and offers music, too. It's a superior site for late-evening conversation.

There's a good selection of imported beers and ales, both on draft and in bottles, and the downstairs fare is an improvement on usual bar offerings. A couple of dinner specials are served each evening, and there's an all-day "stock pot special," a stew of one type or another, served by either the cup or the bowl.

Black bean soup has been outstanding, and Dressel's chili is pretty good too. Grilled fish is properly prepared, and a Spanish-style chicken stew with tomatoes and olives is a lovely winter dish. The Cornish meat pie reflects its heritage, and there's even a bratwurst steamed in beer, then grilled. It's superior.

DUFF'S
392 North Euclid Ave.
361-0522

❖❖❖

Cuisine: Country French
Serves: Dinner, Tuesday–Sunday; lunch, Tuesday–Friday; brunch, Saturday and Sunday
Prices: Moderate to expensive
Credit Cards: All major
Dress: Casual
Reservations: Accepted, advised on weekends
Handicap Access: Satisfactory
Separate No-Smoking Section: Yes

Perhaps the best dining buy for the buck in the area, Duff's has been a Central West End standout since 1972, when, along with next-block neighbor Balaban's, it was one of the several new restaurants that proved instrumental in changing St. Louisans' dining habits.

Casual and inexpensive, the restaurant featured superior meals and an intelligent, well-chosen wine list, both at modest prices, plus mix-and-match furniture, a warm welcome for the few hippies left in the area, and poetry readings on Monday nights.

Those roots are not forgotten. Even with a second dining room to the south almost doubling the space, furniture remains mix-and-match, the service is friendly and casual, and there still are cultural adventures one Monday a month—readings of poetry and prose, along with music.

And the meals are better than ever, at prices that are higher, but still a superior value.

Duff's mails a menu every few months. A couple of the seven or eight entrees seem to be constant presences, others change with the seasons or with tastes. Pepper steak is a perennial, and so is chicken Marsala, but Duff's is a splendid place to experiment.

Over a given year, the menu will include dishes like stuffed Cornish hen, spicy gumbo, duck with cranberries, beef tournedos in choron and marchand de vin sauces, and a wide range of other delights.

Appetizers run the same course. A special favorite is pork tenderloin triangles: smoked tenderloin topped with refried beans, wrapped in philo dough, and baked. And if that weren't good enough by itself, well, it's accompanied by sour cream that has been laced with jalapeño peppers, one of the great dips. Pâtés are excellent. So is the crabmeat quesadilla.

Vegetables are seasonal and prepared just right, and the home-baked breads are delicious.

The wine list is a superior collection of good wines at moderate prices. In addition, there are a couple of wine specials, picked by the highly knowledgeable Tim Kirby to accompany specific menu items in splendid style.

Homemade desserts are exceptional, and Duff's shows off nut pies, like pecan or even cashew, in a glorious manner.

GRAPPA
512 North Euclid Ave.
361-2021

Cuisine: Modern American-Italian
Serves: Lunch and dinner, Monday–Saturday
Prices: Moderate to expensive
Credit Cards: All major
Dress: Informal
Reservations: Accepted
Handicap Access: Satisfactory
Separate No-Smoking Section: Yes

If restaurants had a Rookie of the Year competition, Grappa would have been an easy St. Louis winner in 1991. At the northern edge of the Euclid Avenue strip, it has large windows and a black-and-white tile floor, so it can be on the noisy side. But the overwhelming sound is usually that of cheers for what is emanating from the kitchen of Chef Lou Rook.

The menu is Modern American, but there are Italian and southwestern overtones, and there is a superior use of fresh vegetables to go along with some of the city's more unusual dishes.

Color and presentation are obviously important too. For example, a lamb entree was surrounded by yellow bell peppers, green beans, and carrots. Chicken arrived with mashed potatoes, eggplant, and corn on the cob. No broccoli. No cauliflower. No complaints.

Grappa puts a whole new face on steak tartar—beginning with Limousin beef and using a variety of piquant peppers to give it extra snap. Crab, sausage, and scallion fritters, with a roasted pepper and sweet onion confit, are exemplary, again with contrasting flavors that add a little extra to the dish. Onion soup, based on roasted onions, inspired diverse taste sensations and was a delight.

Entrees, which change with the season, offer the same variety: roasted rabbit, veal shank, pasta with lump crab, pork medallions with papardelle pasta (a wide, flat noodle), free-range chicken, grilled lamb with lamb sausage, and Cornish game hen.

Lamb was rich and delicious, with a hint of rosemary in the sausage and a serving of fresh fig relish that set off the entree to perfection. Chicken was juicy and tender, accompanied by steaming mashed potatoes, and the succulent rabbit was prepared with expertise. Beef tenderloin, with shallot butter and a garlic- thyme potato cake, again evoked superior flavor contrasts in a dish that began with outstanding raw materials and triumphed through perfect preparation. It's a combination that's hard to beat.

The wine list is long and superior, with a special section— probably the best in town—of after-dinner drinks like eau de vie, Armagnac, cognac, port, sherry, Madeira and, of course, the restaurant's namesake, grappa, and its French equivalent, marc.

Desserts are beautifully displayed, and a lemon-blueberry cheesecake was good, though not as memorable as the remainder of the meal, which was truly outstanding.

KOPPERMAN'S
386 North Euclid Ave.
(Central West End)
361-0100

❖❖

Cuisine: Delicatessen, and more
Serves: Breakfast, lunch, and dinner every day; open until midnight on Friday and Saturday
Prices: Moderate
Credit Cards: MC, V
Dress: Casual
Reservations: Not applicable
Handicap Access: Satisfactory
Separate No-Smoking Section: Yes

The Central West End is home to what is probably the best people-watching in the area, and outdoor cafes are the perfect watching place, as generations of Parisians will attest. Of course, the watching in Paris is a lot better than the watching in St. Louis, especially since I think we have only six or seven weeks a year when weather permits the pleasure of outdoor dining.

Kopperman's, a combination of delicatessen, restaurant, wine store, and market, fills the bill nicely, especially at breakfast time, when one can watch the neighborhood come alive.

The restaurant has stretched far beyond the Kosher-style meats and includes outstanding fried chicken and good barbecued ribs, plus superior soups at the lunch and dinner hours. Smoked meats are delicious, there's a wide range of salads and appetizer items, a good reasonably priced wine list, and a nice variety of beers, ales, and soda pops.

LLYWELYN AP GRUFFYD
4747 McPherson Ave.
361-3003

❖-❖

Cuisine: Bar fare, and more
Serves: Lunch and dinner, every day (same menu)
Prices: Inexpensive to moderate
Credit Cards: MC, V
Dress: Casual
Reservations: Not applicable
Handicap Access: Satisfactory
Separate No-Smoking Section: No

Ma Bell's directory assistance operators have more trouble with this number than with any in town; no one can spell *Llywelyn* properly, and it just doesn't exist as "Lou and Ellen's," which some people think is its name.

Jack Brangle, an excellent host and storyteller, has operated it for more than a decade, and his wife, Pat, a fine artist, is responsible for the signs, menu, and some of the tongue-in-cheek artwork inside. Brangle's favorite printable story involves the down-on-his-heels neighborhood denizen who wandered in one day, still hoping it was the Castlewood, which it had been for many years.

Brangle was behind the bar. He listened to the man's hard-luck story and offered him a bowl of chili. He walked to the other end of the bar to order the chili, stopped to talk briefly, and returned with the bowl. The man was gone.

Brangle checked the floor around the stool. Still gone.

"He walked out," another patron reported. "Mumbled something about the lousy service, got off the stool, and walked out."

Llywelyn's chili, which is pretty good for the bar variety, deserves better.

I know the same story is in the book's first edition, but it's too good to leave out. Everything else here will be new, I promise.

The best news about Llywelyn's is that it has expanded, taking over the space next door and knocking a hole in the wall. In addition, there are a new kitchen, new rest rooms, and a new dishwasher, which means one eats off china with stainless-steel utensils, instead of plastic.

The bar-restaurant, which caters to newspaper types and occasional artists and musicians, brought the neighborhood "Welsh Chips," which are fresh-cooked potato chips, thin and crisp and very good. Try the fried onions too; they're not battered but sliced very thin and fried dark and crispy.

Hamburgers are satisfactory, and the rarebit and chili dogs are first-rate. Grilled chicken breast is tasty hot or cold, and so is the Philly Steak in a cheese sauce. The same sauce also works on hot dogs, especially with those fried onions. And an expanded menu is in the works.

The bar has a good selection of imported beer and ale, English hard cider on draft, and plans for some better wines. Domino players can borrow a set to while away a quiet afternoon.

MUSEUM CAFE
St. Louis Art Museum
(Forest Park)
721-5325

❖-❖

Cuisine: Modern American
Serves: Lunch, Tuesday–Saturday; brunch, Sunday
Prices: Inexpensive to moderate
Credit Cards: All major
Dress: Informal
Reservations: Not accepted
Handicap Access: Satisfactory
Separate No-Smoking Section: Yes

The old saw about the food served in art museums being equal to the art hanging in restaurants falls apart in this sunny, second-floor establishment in the St. Louis Art Museum. In fact, given some travel in recent years, lunch at the Museum Cafe here is better than that served in similar museums in Kansas City, New York (the Met), Amsterdam, or Brussels. The Tate Gallery, in London, has the best museum food I know, and the snack bar at the Musée d'Orsay, in Paris, has the best view.

It's a light menu of salads, sandwiches, soups, and a couple of entrees, and everything I've tried has been excellent, providing all the energy needed to traipse the galleries for the remainder of the day.

There's even an international flair with dishes like pork satay with Indonesian spices and peanut sauce, or arancini, a fried Italian rice ball.

Soups are good, and a spinach soup, with a hint of gorgonzola cheese and a little crumbled bacon on top, was exemplary.

Smoked turkey on sourdough bread is a superior sandwich, and potato chips made from sweet potatoes are a great taste sensation.

85

Shrimp and corn enchiladas are splendid, but the blue corn chips served on the side were about as tough as the plate itself. Salads are imaginatively created and extremely tasty.

Desserts are winners too, with apple-cranberry crisp a highlight.

NANTUCKET COVE
40 North Kingshighway
361-0625

❖❖❖

Cuisine: Seafood
Serves: Dinner, Monday–Saturday
Prices: Moderate to expensive
Credit Cards: All major
Dress: Informal (jackets preferred)
Reservations: Accepted
Handicap Access: Satisfactory
Separate No-Smoking Section: Yes

Nantucket Cove is a throwback to the days when seafood meant New England, and restaurants that specialized in fish had to look like New England fish houses: beamed ceilings, nets and buoys here and there, treasure-map menus when cute was in style, and a tank or two to hold the lobsters.

And lo, these many years later, when fresh seafood is available at every good restaurant in the nation, thanks to air freight and dining habits that joined mine, Nantucket Cove remains a seafood house in the old style.

And it's still a dependable place to dine. It is not a great restaurant, and modern cooking styles are barred at the door, but Nantucket Cove handles the basics in fine style, with dependable preparation and friendly servers, some of whom may have been here throughout the establishment's tenure of nearly thirty years.

There are a couple of steaks on the menu, but the specialty is seafood, headed by lobster and including both salt- and fresh-water residents. The oyster bar at the front door is a busy place, especially during cocktail hour when they are discounted, but those who want something better and go inside for dinner will have Blue Points, while the bar serves bivalves from the Gulf. There's a difference, too.

Lobsters have been excellent through the years; they're expensive, but hardly anything beats a freshly steamed lobster for dinner. Those who go early can find some bargains. Grilled salmon also was successful, but other entrees were uneven, some arriving overcooked, others undercooked.

Salads are quite good, boasting the original Mayfair dressing—a St. Louis classic that was created when Gordon Heiss operated both Nantucket Cove and the Mayfair Room many years ago. It's a creamy anchovy dressing, very familiar in restaurants everywhere today, but there still seems to be something special about it at the Cove.

Both baked and french fried potatoes, plus rice, are available; and the fries were fine, but the last baked potato I had was undercooked and rock-hard—something that just shouldn't happen. Nantucket Cove has boasted of its cornbread for years, and deservedly so. It's excellent.

The wine list is very strong on whites, less so on reds, but the proportion is proper for a fish house and the selection is good.

Pecan pie seems to be the proper dessert; Nantucket Cove's version is extremely rich and very sweet, revealing a heavy hand with the corn syrup.

REDEL'S
310 DeBaliviere
367-7005

❖◦❖

Cuisine: American
Serves: Dinner, every day; lunch, Monday–Friday
Prices: Moderate to expensive
Credit Cards: AE, MC, V
Dress: Casual
Reservations: Accepted for parties of five or more
Handicap Access: Satisfactory
Separate No-Smoking Section: Yes

Trying to classify the style of cuisine at Lee Redel's friendly, casual restaurant is an impossible task. I began with "American Modern," thereby granting full citizenship to pizza, which probably deserves it by now. But what's modern about fried chicken, salmon croquettes, or prime rib?

That's old-fashioned American, but there's nothing old-fashioned about Redel's, where a good California influence is strong in a wide range of imaginatively prepared, tasty, and satisfying meals.

Take the salmon croquettes, or salmon cakes as the menu calls them. They're made of fresh salmon, nicely spiced, fried to be crisp on the edges, and served with cream gravy and peas. No! Just kidding. They come with a wonderfully tangy sauce alongside, bolstered with a nifty touch of cayenne, and they may just be the best salmon croquettes I've ever tasted.

I'm not a great fan of butcher paper and crayons on tables, though many football coaches of my acquaintance would be entranced. Problem is that their diagrams would take up so much space that there would be no room for the plates.

The menu offers something for almost everyone, with seasonal

89

specials featuring fresh seafood and produce. The pizza is splendid, with a thin crust and a choice of toppings limited only by the imagination. Prime rib is good, and the fried chicken is wonderful. There are also some seafood specials, barbecued ribs, steaks, and teriyaki-marinated items like outstanding grilled shrimp. Appetizers run a similar range, including mussels, crab Rangoon, pâté, and ceviche.

In the soup category, Redel's black bean is outstanding, arriving rich and hot and very tasty, thick with delicious black beans, onions, and a superior additional touch of spicy sausage. Lobster bisque, with a touch of cayenne, is exceptional. Mussels, in a very garlicky, Provençal-style, tomato-filled broth, are excellent. The house salad is fresh and crisp, and the blue cheese dressing is delicious.

The wine list is mostly of recent vintages but has excellent, moderately priced selections. Desserts, led by a powerful, whiskey-aided bread pudding, are superior. Besides, how can you you not like a restaurant whose menu notes, "We don't care if it is your birthday"?

SANSUI
4955 West Pine Blvd.
367-2020

✦✦

Cuisine: Japanese
Serves: Dinner, Monday–Saturday; lunch, Monday–Friday
Prices: Moderate (expensive if you go wild on sushi)
Credit Cards: AE, MC, V
Dress: Informal
Reservations: Accepted
Handicap Access: Satisfactory
Separate No-Smoking Section: No

A sushi bar is as dangerous to me as a cocktail bar to an alcoholic. Normally a responsible, decorous, upstanding citizen, I find myself sitting at the bar, admiring the chef's talents and babbling, "That's right, one more of those, and another of that one, and maybe two of that over there."

I love the taste and texture varieties of the raw fish, be it flounder or yellowtail or tuna or squid. I love the chilled rice and the fiery green horseradish, though I treat the latter with extreme respect. I am filled with awe as the chef slices and wraps and folds and twists.

And suddenly, because sushi is not inexpensive, I discover that my stomach is full and my wallet empty.

Sushi has another special quality. It may be one of the few foods I love that is low in both calories and cholesterol, or so I've read. I don't always believe the eating advice I read (sometimes I don't even believe the eating advice I write), but I believe it about sushi.

Sansui, a small, neat Central West End restaurant, serves excellent sushi. Tempura has been very good, and on occasion, the rich, beef-and-vegetable laden stew cooked at tableside and known as sukiyaki has been outstanding. On other visits, very tough meat

91

was the problem. Other dishes have been inconsistent, not a good quality in a restaurant, and there are service flaws, too. But when the urge for sushi is strong, Sansui comes through.

SHALIMAR GARDEN
4569 Laclede Ave.
361-6911

Cuisine: Indian
Serves: Dinner, every day; lunch, Monday–Saturday
Prices: Moderate to expensive
Credit Cards: MC, V
Dress: Informal
Reservations: Accepted
Handicap Access: Satisfactory
Separate No-Smoking Section: No

Shalimar Garden has been on the St. Louis restaurant scene almost as long as I have. I first wrote about it when it was next door to a coin laundry in a contiguous suburb, and I have followed it through Maplewood on its way to the Central West End, where it settled in 1987, in the neighborhood probably best suited to it.

The fare is Indian, and when the server asks, "Mild, medium or hot?" think about it a little. "Hot" at Shalimar is incendiary. It's a white heat that fries the palate and sears the throat, makes sweat pop out on the forehead, and clears the sinuses in an instant.

Not everything is fiery of course. Some dishes are always mild, and the cooks here can prepare dishes to the diner's desire. I ask for somewhere between medium and hot, and it works for me. Indian spicing, unlike that of, say, jalapeño peppers, blazes but doesn't last too long.

If it burns fiercely, try the raita, or cucumber-yogurt relish. It's very cooling. The chapati, a bread much like pita, or the naan, a fried bread, also works to absorb the heat. The Indian breads are wonderful, and I'm fond of them all, but most fond of the papadam, a paper-thin, crisp, melt-in-your-mouth fried lentil flour variety, with some coriander here and there to add some pop.

93

Appetizers include samosas—turnovers filled with seasoned meat or potatoes—and they're excellent. A fried puff pastry, served with spicy yogurt, is nice before a meal, too.

Most of the entrees involve chicken or lamb with a curry sauce, and that's where the big decisions on heat come in. The meat and sauce arrive in one bowl, with rice (white or brown) or vegetables in another. One ladles meat and sauce atop rice or vegetables, then digs in.

Chicken is tender, lamb less so, and therein lies my major problem with Shalimar. Not enough attention is paid to raw materials, and lamb can be very fatty on occasion.

An interesting dish is nargisi kofta, cousin to what the English call a Scotch egg. It's a hard-boiled egg wrapped in ground beef, then battered and fried; but the Indian version's beef and accompanying spices are more tangy, and more flavorful as well.

Chutney and lemon-rind pickles come alongside, but even the sweet chutney can be fiery hot.

Desserts involve mango or rice pudding, and gulab jamun, a very sweet ball of cooked dough served in an even sweeter honey sauce.

SUNSHINE INN
8½ South Euclid Ave.
367-1413

❖❖❖

Cuisine: American vegetarian (some fish and chicken dishes)
Serves: Lunch and dinner, Tuesday–Sunday; brunch, Saturday and Sunday
Prices: Inexpensive to moderate
Credit Cards: MC, V
Dress: Casual
Reservations: Accepted
Handicap Access: Satisfactory
Separate No-Smoking Section: Yes

Dinner at the Sunshine Inn is filling and inexpensive. It isn't as purely vegetarian as it once was, with chicken and fish dishes now on the menu, but it remains an excellent dining value, with some first-rate, imaginative methods of food preparation, plus wine and beer, and a great tradition of superior desserts.

Salads are splendid, and the kitchen now shows a nice touch with dishes in the Mexican and Chinese style, including some of the best-prepared tofu in the city.

I'm sometimes puzzled by the selection of vegetables, which seems mostly limited to standards like broccoli, cauliflower, zucchini, carrots, and so on. I'd like to see braised celery, or fresh beets, or even brussels sprouts. On my visits to the Sunshine Inn, I've been disappointed by finding the same vegetables as at every other restaurant in town, and nothing different or special.

Still, the stir-frying techniques are excellent, and the use of herbs shows a nice touch.

Stuffed mushrooms are an exceptional appetizer and the soups are good—especially the white bean. Chili con queso is also nicely spiced.

Salads are huge and delicious, with homemade dressings to match. Vegetarian burgers seem to be an item for specific tastes. Scallops are good, and so are several varieties of quiche.

It isn't a dinner dish, but the Sunshine Inn's date-nut bread with cream cheese is a spectacular item, and it's topped with fresh fruit that provides both eye and taste appeal.

The wine list is small, but has a few nice bottles that are good accompaniments. You must save room for the carrot cake, a long-time favorite that is sweetened with honey and molasses for a different flavor. The ice cream desserts are giant-sized and immediately replace all the calories saved by eating in a vegetarian manner.

TOM'S BAR & GRILL
20 South Euclid Ave.
367-4900

‣‣

Cuisine: Bar fare
Serves: Lunch and dinner every day (same menu)
Prices: Inexpensive to moderate
Credit Cards: MC, V
Dress: Casual
Reservations: Not applicable
Handicap Access: Satisfactory
Separate No-Smoking Section: No

A large A-frame room with a huge skylight is the centerpiece of Tom's Bar & Grill. A fireplace makes it even more attractive, and it's fun to watch the sun set—or the snow come down.

The food is basic Central West End bar fare of hamburgers, chicken wings, soups, and chili, all passable and filling, and I find Tom's a pleasant lunch stop during the work week.

SOUTH

South of Forest Park and west to the city limits, including restaurants located in the Hill and Dogtown neighborhoods and on Gravois Road, South Grand Boulevard, South Kingshighway, Hampton Avenue, Watson Road, and a few other thoroughfares.

Agusti's (Hill)
Amighetti's Bakery (Hill)
The Bavarian Inn (Gravois)
Bella Pasta (Hampton)
Bevo Mill (Gravois)
Blue Water Grill (Hampton)
Cafe de Manila (Grand)
Charlie Gitto's on the Hill (Hill)
Chuy's (Dogtown)
Cunetto House of Pasta (Hill)
Despina's (Morganford Road)
Dogtown Bistro (Dogtown)
Dominic's (Hill)
Fao Mai (Grand)
Gian-Peppe's (Hill)
Gian-Tony's (Hill)
Gino's (Hampton)

Giovanni's (Hill)
Giuseppe's (Grand)
Guidry's Cajun Restaurant (very far south)
Hunan Cafe (Hampton)
The King and I (Grand)
LoRusso's (Watson)
O'Connell's Pub (Kingshighway)
Olympia Kebab House and Taverna (McCausland)
Pat's Bar & Grill (Dogtown)
Pho Grand (Grand)
Sam's St. Louis Steak House (Gravois)
Slider's (Hampton)
Spiro's (Watson)
Uncle Bill's Pancake House (Kingshighway)

AGUSTI'S

2300 Edwards St.
(The Hill)
772-6003

❖❖❖

Cuisine: Italian
Serves: Dinner, Tuesday–Sunday
Prices: Moderate
Credit Cards: All major
Dress: Informal
Reservations: Accepted
Handicap Access: Satisfactory
Separate No-Smoking Section: Yes

On the site of the venerated Ruggeri's, where steak was king and sports figures were in regular attendance, Agusti's has made a home for good Italian fare, moderately priced, nicely served, and coming from the kitchen with a touch of imagination.

Pastas and basic Italian veal and chicken dishes are nicely prepared and properly served, and there's a friendly aura to the operation.

As a longtime nonfan of toasted ravioli, but as one who tastes it out of dedication to duty, I was pleasantly surprised at the dish here. The crust was thin and tasty, the filling nicely spiced, and the overall effect excellent.

Appetizers, in addition to the ravioli, include a first-rate fritto misto (literally, mixed fry), a large collection of fresh vegetables lightly battered, quickly fried, and served piping hot.

The pasta selection is large, and includes a fine version of classic fettuccine Alfredo, plus some excellent linguine with chicken livers, a personal favorite and most welcome here because the livers were cooked just right, juicy and flavorful.

Restaurants like Agusti's are prevalent in the Hill area—large portions of well-prepared traditional dishes, mostly from southern Italy—and each has its fans and regular customers. They're an asset to the community.

·AMIGHETTI'S BAKERY

5141 Wilson Ave. (The Hill) **776-2855**

101 North Broadway (Downtown) **241-3700**

1010 Market St. (Downtown) **241-8555**

8000 Carondelet Ave. (Mid-County) **725-8081**

9872 Watson Rd. (Mid-County) **966- 8676**

Cuisine: Italian, primarily sandwiches
Serves: Lunch and early dinner, Tuesday–Saturday (same menu)
Prices: Inexpensive to moderate
Credit Cards: None at Hill location; AE, MC, V at others
Dress: Casual
Reservations: Not applicable
Handicap Access: Satisfactory
Separate No-Smoking Section: No

Marge Amighetti—another St. Louis legend—began with a bakery on the Hill, long the city's Italian enclave. In time, she started filling some extra loaves with meats and cheeses from the neighborhood's splendid delicatessens. Call 'em Poor Boys, Subs, or Heroes, they have always been a tasty, filling lunch, and for several generations, St. Louisans have lined up in the store, and onto the street, for their carry-out delights.

A few sidewalk tables were added, and then an interior expansion provided even more room for hungry lunchers. In 1986, a downtown branch was opened, with a similar menu and identical sandwiches. More locations followed, and there are those who feel quality and personality have slipped because of mass-production techniques.

The Amighetti Special, laden with meat and cheese of all types, remains a most popular item. For those who want slightly less, there are all sorts of other combinations, limited only by the appetite and the imagination.

And if you just want delicious loaves of crusty bread, the location on the Hill still provides them.

THE BAVARIAN INN
3016 Arsenal Street
(South Side)
771-7755

Cuisine: German
Serves: Lunch and dinner, Monday–Saturday
Prices: Inexpensive to moderate
Credit Cards: All major
Dress: Informal
Reservations: Accepted
Handicap Access: Satisfactory
Separate No-Smoking Section: No

For a city with a strong German heritage, St. Louis has a disappointingly small number of German restaurants and none that are outstanding. Maybe people of German extraction cook and eat at home. However, the Bavarian Inn has stood for many years as a location for adequate, consistent meals at modest prices. Not great food, but filling and satisfying when the urge strikes.

The sausage selection is fine, and the wurst is generally excellent, even if the sauerkraut and red cabbage have the aura of commercial preparation. Let's grant that I have a soft spot for wurst of all types; I love the spicy combinations of beef, pork, and veal, whether steamed or grilled, and topped with some tangy horseradish.

Wienerschnitzel and sauerbraten are available, usually satisfactory, though the veal cutlet tends to be superior to the pot roast.

Spaetzle, or dumplings, often are on the menu, and they're pleasant; fried potatoes have been first-rate.

Strudel is so-so, and on the heavy side, but there's a good selection of German beer, and when the mood is for German cooking, the Bavarian Inn can leave one pleasantly filled.

BELLA PASTA
3453 Hampton Ave.
351-8812

❖❖

Cuisine: Italian
Serves: Dinner, Monday–Saturday; lunch, Monday–Friday
Prices: Moderate
Credit Cards: All major
Dress: Casual
Reservations: Accepted
Handicap Access: Difficult (space limited)
Separate No-Smoking Section: No

This tiny space in a small, street-corner shopping center now has been home to two outstanding restaurants, both Italian and both excellent, though they offer different dishes. Bella Pasta moved in some 2½ years ago, after LoRusso's left for larger quarters, and proved again that good things do come in small packages.

The small menu, bolstered by a handful of daily specials, shows many familiar Italian dishes, but the imaginative use of spices and herbs gives them an individual touch that is elegantly different.

Crostini, a perfect companion to a predinner drink, involves some delicious toppings—sweet roasted peppers, salmon, anchovies, several cheeses—for crisp, toasted Italian bread. Caponata, with eggplant and peppers in larger-than-usual chunks, is more for the fork than as a dip, but it's delicious, with nice flavors of garlic and olive oil.

Pesto sauce, or simple oil and garlic, are superior pasta sauces, and veal piccata, a simple dish, is heightened by the substitution of shiitake mushrooms for buttons. Chicken carron, a broiled breast with prosciutto and porcini mushrooms, is an elegant combination of flavors.

Bluefish, grilled simply, and to perfection, was a delight. I love

105

bluefish, which has a rich, delicious, fishy flavor. There are those who complain about fish that tastes fishy, and I wonder why they order fish in the first place.

The wine list is small, but includes some moderately priced bottles from Kendall-Jackson and Gundlach-Bundschu, good producers of California table wines.

The dessert list begins and ends—for me—with zabaglione that is as good as any I've ever eaten. A dollop of caramel in the bottom of the snifter is a great beginning, and the sugar–egg yolk–wine mixture is whipped frothy and poured over it. Some fresh fruit, like strawberries or blueberries in season, is tossed on top and swirled lightly, adding color, texture, and flavor. A brilliant dessert.

Bella Pasta is a very small restaurant, often crowded and occasionally noisy. The kitchen is open, the service good, and the meals outstanding.

BEVO MILL
4749 Gravois
(South Side)
481-2626

Cuisine: American, some German dishes
Serves: Lunch and dinner, every day; brunch on Sunday
Prices: Moderate to expensive
Credit Cards: All major
Dress: Informal
Reservations: Accepted
Handicap Access: Satisfactory
Separate No-Smoking Section: No

Long a south St. Louis landmark, with windmilled and often-overdone decor, the Bevo Mill dates to the beginning of the century, when an early August Busch decided that a German restaurant would help beer sales.

It may be kind of kitschy, but the Bevo (as St. Louisans call it), remains warm and comfortable, even if the cuisine is not what it once was.

Now part of the Pat Hanon–Ray Gallardo restaurant group, meals have improved, but they have a long way to go.

A few German basics highlight the menu, which also includes grilled fish and chicken, steaks, and chops that are standards on the often-trendy menus of the group's other establishments.

Portions tend to be large and on the bland side, and the prime rib has many fans.

The windmill and the decor still make it worth a journey with out-of-town visitors.

BLUE WATER GRILL
2607 Hampton Ave.
645-0707

❖❖

Cuisine: Southwestern (tapas on Monday nights)
Serves: Dinner, Monday–Saturday; lunch, Monday–Friday
Prices: Moderate to expensive
Credit Cards: All major
Dress: Informal
Reservations: Accepted only for parties of six or more
Handicap Access: Difficult (narrow aisles)
Separate No-Smoking Section: Smoking only in bar area

Hampton Avenue begins at Forest Park and goes just about due south until it ends at the River des Peres. It forms the western edge of the Hill, and in the last decade, it has become home to a large number of restaurants, mostly small and casual, many of them very good.

In the area where the Hill rises sharply to the east, there are many Italian restaurants, as if they slipped off the Hill and settled where they landed along Hampton Avenue. But the star of the Hampton strip is the Blue Water Grill, where a talented kitchen, under the leadership of Tim Mallett, brings forth exemplary Southwestern fare, and, on Monday nights, provides splendid tapas, with proper touches of both Spain and Mexico.

The regular menu is divided into Small Plates, Bowls, Salads, Fresh Fish, and Large Plates, providing something for everyone and a nifty opportunity to plan a dinner of the proper size.

Chipotles, anchos, green chiles, and cilantro are common spices, and there's hoisin and ginger for some dishes. Mexican chorizo and New Orleans andouille sausages add their particular spicing, and there's a generous hand with garlic.

The result is meals with superb flavor combinations; rarely is anything overspiced, but almost everything is piquant and delicious.

The menu changes seasonally, and there are always daily specials. Some of the winning appetizers include wild mushrooms in puff pastry with chipotle sauce, chicken quesadillas with guacamole and chorizo, and shrimp bisque with the lovely addition of fresh tomato.

It may be passé in some places, but blackened redfish is delicious when it's cooked right—and it's cooked right here. Grilled salmon with soy and ginger, topped with hoisin butter, is a superb blend of barely tangy tastes, and so is grilled chicken, well rubbed with rosemary and served with a light green chile sauce.

Grilled, thinly sliced potatoes are excellent, but too often underdone, and jicama, a crispy root vegetable with a little spice, is a nice accompaniment.

On tapas night, there are cold and hot dishes, usually in servings like dim sum, a good sample for two people. Some of the dishes are served in large entree-sized portions.

My favorite cold dishes include white and black bean salad with chorizo and spicy shrimp; a Spanish style omelet with scallops; herb-grilled potato salad with chipotle mayonnaise and chorizo; and chilled grilled swordfish on sweet-and-sour cabbage.

Hot dishes I cannot resist include a seafood quesadilla; corn and crabmeat griddle cake; seafood chowder with saffron; shrimp stuffed with crabmeat and cornbread; chicken wrapped in cornbread; steamed clams with lemon, garlic, and butter; baked oysters with creamed spinach and Cajun spices; and grilled squid with lemon and garlic.

The Blue Water wine list is passable, well chosen to go with spicy meals, and there are always several good Australian labels along with mostly standard California ones.

Desserts, made in house, include a chocolate enchilada filled with whipped cream and fresh fruit that is now delicious. At one time, the enchilada was fried, and it was served with a steak knife. Enough said! Apple, caramel, and pecan pie also score well.

CAFE DE MANILA
3161 South Grand Blvd.
773-5997

❖❖❖

Cuisine: Filipino
Serves: Dinner, Monday–Saturday; lunch, Monday–Friday; brunch, Sunday
Prices: Moderate
Credit Cards: AE, MC, V
Dress: Informal
Reservations: Accepted
Handicap Access: Satisfactory
Separate No-Smoking Section: No

First opened as part of a grocery in a small south-side store, the Cafe de Manila's excellent Filipino cuisine, and the fact that it was the only game in town, led to expansion to a larger, more stylish location on South Grand Boulevard, in the heart of a burgeoning area for Asian restaurants of all persuasions.

Filipino cuisine often has French or Spanish overtones and always delicate, unusual spicing, quite different from that of its Asian neighbors. Dishes are not overly spicy, but show a lovely touch with herbs and some taste experiences far from the local norm.

For example, there are three types of lumpia, the Filipino equivalent of egg roll—very different and delicious. Lumpia sariwa, or fresh lumpia, is a fat roll of sautéd shrimp, jicamas, and other vegetables in a thin, crêpelike wrapper, with a garlicky, peppery peanut sauce on the side. Lumpia de Manila is about the thickness of a cigar with the filling more finely ground and the whole thing deep-fried, crisp, and dry. Lumpia Frito is more like the traditional Chinese egg roll, but is all- vegetable.

Escargot, also delicious, is prepared in a manner far from the classic French. They arrive in a sauce that blends coconut milk, garlic, and butter for a nutty, delightful flavor.

Entrees include some skewered items, one with pickled green papaya and a choice of shrimp or pork poached in tamarind juice. Several dishes are prepared in sugar cane vinegar and soy sauce, or in coconut milk, and there's a curried chicken too.

Roast duck in mango sauce, served with slices of the juicy fruit, is delicious, and a breast of chicken in vinegar and soy has a delicate, slightly marinated flavor that is outstanding. Pork is prepared in the same manner and is equally good. Shrimp rellenado involves fat shrimp that are wrapped with lightly spiced ground beef, then wrapped again in thin pastry and deep fried. The result is sensational.

While the food is not spicy, many dishes are served with dipping sauces that have a solid bite, which makes it easy to be experimental, and at low risk, too.

CHARLIE GITTO'S ON THE HILL
5226 Shaw Ave.
(The Hill)
772-8898

Cuisine: Italian
Serves: Dinner every day; lunch, Monday–Friday
Prices: Moderate to expensive
Credit Cards: AE, MC, V
Dress: Informal
Reservations: Accepted
Handicap Access: Satisfactory
Separate No-Smoking Section: No

Major remodeling and an upgrade in the kitchen have made this longtime Hill standout a more pleasant dining experience and a better value, while it remains a solid, late- night favorite for sports figures with postgame appetites.

The antipasto platter is a work of tasty art, and the veal and chicken dishes, under traditional and classic sauces of Sicilian derivation, are first-rate. So is the selection of steaks and chops. Service is black-tie and generally excellent.

Pastas and salads are fresh and tasty, and the kitchen seems smoother than it used to be. The patio is gone, however, in favor of a lovely banquet room with a view of the outdoors. It's not quite as nice, but safe from rain, heat, and cold.

CHUY'S
6405 Clayton Ave.
644-4430

Cuisine: Mexican
Serves: Dinner, Tuesday–Sunday; lunch, Tuesday–Friday
Prices: Inexpensive
Credit Cards: MC, Visa
Dress: Casual
Reservations: Not Accepted
Handicap Access: Satisfactory
Separate No-Smoking Section: No

The Dogtown neighborhood, just south of Forest Park, doesn't exist as far as the city of St. Louis is concerned. For some reason—political correctness perhaps—the Community Development Agency has eliminated the venerable neighborhood, renaming part of it as Clayton-Tamm and incorporating the rest into Hypointe and Franz Park. The CDA doesn't know that Hi-Pointe is the preferred spelling.

The CDA also doesn't know that Dogtown residents are proud to live there. The origin of the name is lost in history, but the most popular, and most entertaining, is that the Igorot Indians camped there during the 1904 World's Fair and that the neighborhood dogs disappeared rather rapidly.

Today there are no more Igorots, and a normal supply of dogs, and some nifty little neighborhood bars and bistros amid the comfortable, well-kept homes.

Chuy's, one of the city's best restaurant bargains, is small and plain, in a brightly lighted storefront. But it turns out the best fajitas (either beef or chicken) in the city and spectacular, fork-mixed guacamole that has superior flavor and texture. Salsa has a tongue-tingling piquancy, and nachos are excellent, with individual chips and not a gooey mass.

Enchiladas are first-rate, tacos less so, but the chalupas are good and so are the refried beans.

CUNETTO HOUSE OF PASTA
5453 Magnolia Ave.
(The Hill)
781-1135

❖–❖

Cuisine: Italian
Serves: Dinner, Monday–Saturday; lunch, Monday–Friday
Prices: Inexpensive to moderate
Credit Cards: All major
Dress: Informal
Reservations: Accepted only for lunch
Handicap Access: Satisfactory
Separate No-Smoking Section: No

The pasta is generally splendid and the prices are remarkably low—a combination that makes this one of the busiest restaurants in the city. But be prepared to wait at least a half-hour, and usually more, because of the no-reservation policy at dinner.

Pasta is the specialty, with a wide range of noodle types and sauces that usually are bright, tasty, and rich, but there are some other traditional Italian dishes that are well made. Eggplant Parmigiana is one of my favorites.

Service is good, and the restaurant is hectic, family-filled, and often noisy. But it's an outstanding value, and St. Louisans have recognized that fact for more than a decade.

DESPINA'S
3157 Morganford Rd.
776-5990

Cuisine: American with European overtones
Serves: Dinner, Monday–Saturday; lunch, Monday–Friday
Prices: Moderate
Credit Cards: MC, Visa
Dress: Informal
Reservations: Accepted
Handicapped Access: Satisfactory
Separate No-Smoking Section: Yes

Despina's is the kind of restaurant that is difficult to classify. A charming place just south of Tower Grove Park with tablecloths, fresh flowers, and overtones of gray and mauve in the decorations, it provides good meals at moderate prices, with a touch of elegance in the dining room and a nice display of imagination in the kitchen.

The cuisine has a European flavor, with both Italy and France evident in some of the sauces, and Southwestern influences here and there.

For example, escargots in puff pastry were outstanding, with a sauce of garlic and a little tomato improving them even more. Onion soup, with melted Swiss cheese, was superior.

Homemade salad dressings, either buttermilk or blue cheese, are light and flavorful and help the crisp greens considerably. Spinach salad, with a sweet-and-tangy mustard dressing, is a happy change of pace.

Chicken with lobster tail is stuffed and poached, then sliced into an imaginative, tasty entree. Pepper steak is a winner, and so is pasta in seafood sauce. Vegetables, even broccoli, were properly cooked to the peak of flavor.

Desserts were lackluster, but there has been time for improvement.

DOGTOWN BISTRO
6335 Clayton Ave.
(Dogtown)
645-7722

<hr>

Cuisine: Italian
Serves: Lunch and dinner, Monday–Saturday
Prices: Inexpensive to moderate
Credit Cards: MC, V
Dress: Casual
Reservations: Not applicable
Handicap Access: Satisfactory
Separate No-Smoking Section: No

Another of the many small restaurants and bars that keep the area humming, the Dogtown Bistro is a basic Italian restaurant, small enough to cook to order, large enough to experiment here and there, and inexpensive enough to be a superior value.

Pizza, pasta, and some veal and chicken dishes lead the menu, with an excellent eggplant Parmigiana appetizer and someone in the kitchen who makes winning soups. A lobster bisque one day was a rich, delicious winner, more like a seafood chowder, with chunks of lobster, tiny shrimp and a stock that was hearty and flavorful.

Old-fashioned meatballs and spaghetti is a classic dish, and it's handled here in elegant style.

Roast beef is a favorite, and there are well-stuffed, excellent sandwiches for lunch.

DOMINIC'S
5101 Wilson Ave.
(The Hill)
771-1632

✦✦✦

Cuisine: Italian
Serves: Dinner, Monday–Saturday
Prices: Expensive to very expensive
Credit Cards: All major
Dress: Jackets and ties requested
Reservations: Accepted, advised on weekends
Handicap Access: Satisfactory (few steps at entrance)
Separate No-Smoking Section: No

St. Louis is a city where loyalty is a topic not really worth talking about. It's there, and it's obvious. St. Louis is a city where baseball fans support the Cardinals in good years and bad, where the sporting media sing the praises of every athlete (until he leaves town), and where diners will go to the wall to defend their favorite places.

I was cognizant of this but didn't realize the depth of feeling until I edited the St. Louis edition of a Zagat restaurant guide a few years ago and—inadvertently, believe me—Dominic's was omitted from the ballot.

The screams of anger ricocheted around my head like a swarm of hornets, and I still hear occasional nasty comments.

Giovanni Galati, known as Dominic, never said a word, an action typical of that gentleman and as stylish as his restaurant, one of the very best Italian operations in the city.

Like so many other Italian restaurateurs in the city, Galati used to work at Tony's. When he joined the staff, however, a Giovanni and a John (the Anglicized version) already worked there, and since Vince Bommarito prefers that each waiter at Tony's have a different first name, Giovanni became Dominic.

Some years later, when he decided to open his own restaurant, in the heart of the Hill, Giovanni Galati retained the nom de waiter. In those days, he and his wife, Jackie, lived upstairs above the establishment, and her mother was a prominent, and valued, figure in the kitchen.

Over the years, Dominic's has grown and prospered; it is on the expensive and formal side, but it serves elegant fare with decor and service that match perfectly. Sauces are lighter and there have been more seafood offerings in recent years, but herbs and spices are scattered masterfully, and when a sauce is supposed to be rich, you can count on it.

The menu is strong on classics, but there are some off-menu specials that demonstrate the lighter style.

Cold stuffed mussels are a brilliant appetizer and so are hot ones in either hearty marinara or simple white wine sauce. Shrimp de Jonghe at Dominic's shows a little less garlic and a little more fresh tomato than many other restaurants; the slight change is delicious. Soups are superior too, and one night something described simply as "fish soup" turned out to be gloriously rich and hearty, with overtones of both cioppino and bouillabaise.

Pastas, prepared fresh and perfectly al dente, may be ordered either as appetizers, entrees, or can be split as a side dish with dinner. The homemade ravioli, in either cream or meat sauce, are spectacular, and fettuccine with cream and smoked salmon is another delicious choice.

Gnocchi, a pasta made of potato, but more of a dumpling in my opinion, is excellent. Trenette, a noodle similar to fettucine, is brilliant with pesto sauce.

Entrees include spiedini, or veal rolled and filled with a stuffing showing a touch of prosciutto ham for added flavor, or delicate beef tenderloin sliced and served in a traditional, delicious Marsala sauce.

Simple broiled steaks or rack of lamb with a hint of olive oil and rosemary are just right, and the Dover sole will please any seafood lover. Vegetables are fresh, lightly cooked, and crisp.

The wine list is lengthy and displays a solid selection of Italian varieties.

Desserts are good, and the specialty is "Jackie's Dessert," a custard dish with lots of cinnamon and nuts. Homemade cannoli or cassata cake also are splendid.

Dominic's is expensive, but worth it.

FAO MAI
3216 South Grand Blvd.
772-9988

◆━◆

Cuisine: Vietnamese
Serves: Lunch and dinner, every day
Prices: Inexpensive to moderate
Credit Cards: All major
Dress: Informal
Reservations: Accepted
Handicapped Access: Satisfactory
Separate No-Smoking Area: No

The French influence on Vietnamese cuisine is a natural one—France dominated Southeast Asia for centuries, and French customs and cuisine became part of the norm. For example, the late, great DuBois Chen, who made the St. Louis Trader Vic's the best in the nation for many years, learned to cook in the French navy.

Therefore, finding French touches on the Vietnamese menu in the lovely little Fao Mai is not surprising, though French pastries for dessert are a little unusual. There's an explanation for that, too, because the chef-owner studied cooking in Paris.

The small, storefront restaurant, in the midst of the South Grand strip of Asiatic culture, has a calm, yet very stylish decor, and a large menu involving many types of noodles: some wide and flat and made with eggs, some thin and almost translucent and made of rice flour, and others made of whole wheat. They are served soft or crisp, and they all are very tasty.

Most dishes have lovely flavor but not a lot of fire, though a chili sauce on the table will singe your eyebrows. It's great, for example, with the Fao Mai egg roll, about half the size and half the thickness of a Chinese one. A tangy vinegar sauce accompanies several other appetizers, with piquant pork, shrimp, or vegetables rolled in rice paper or lettuce.

Paper-thin crêpes of rice flour are wrapped around chicken, or pork, or a Vietnamese pâté, providing a different sensation of flavor and texture. Soups, with those thin, thin noodles, are hot and tasty.

Table-grilled beef is similar in preparation to the Japanese sukiyaki or Korean bulgoki, with the diner cooking his or her own. At Fao Mai, the beef is deliciously marinated, sliced paper thin to cook quickly, rolled in a rice-flour pancake with lettuce and cucumbers, and eaten like an enchilada.

Curried chicken brings onions, carrots, celery, and other vegetables, and a rich, balanced curry tang, and salted stir-fried shrimp is delicious.

Service is quick and friendly, and a real effort is made to make sure that Americans' questions about the menu and the cuisine get a proper answer.

The supply and selection of French desserts varies, but if it's on hand, try the exemplary chocolate mousse cake, with dark chocolate on top and both white and dark chocolate mousse in between. The rich, dark, Vietnamese coffee, served over ice and condensed milk, remains one of my favorite drinks.

GIAN-PEPPE'S
2126 Marconi Ave.
(The Hill)
772-3303

❖-❖

Cuisine: Italian
Serves: Dinner, Tuesday–Saturday; lunch, Tuesday–Friday
Prices: Expensive
Credit Cards: AE, MC, V
Dress: Informal (jacket required)
Reservations: Accepted, advised on weekends
Handicap Access: Satisfactory
Separate No-Smoking Section: No

Italian immigrants to St. Louis in the late 19th century congregated on the northern edge of downtown and on a slight rise of ground in the southwest part of the city. The Italian enclave is long gone from downtown, but the Hill remains home to many people of Italian heritage. The area was the boyhood home of Joe Garagiola and Yogi Berra, as every St. Louisan knows; its fire hydrants display the red-green-white of the Italian flag, and the small homes that line its quiet streets have lawns so neat they might have been trimmed with manicure scissors.

St. Ambrose Church long has been the spiritual heart of the Hill, and practically in its shadow is Gian-Peppe's, a small, excellent restaurant where the fare is splendid, the service superior, and the aura most pleasant.

Gian-Peppe's, though in the same culinary class, isn't quite as elegant as its Hill neighbors like Dominic's and Giovanni's, but it provides superior fare in the Italian manner. The menu isn't that different from the city's other first-line Italian spots, but classic dishes, like classic stories, bear repeating.

And Gian-Peppe's, like any other fine restaurant, adds its own touches, like a grilled shrimp appetizer where the crustaceans are lightly breaded with coarse crumbs, then cooked with garlic, butter, and a touch of wine. They're juicy and delicious, with all the flavors perfectly in place.

Mussels, served in a light and flavorful tomato sauce heightened with garlic, are fat and delicious, and fried squid arrives hot, crisp, and dry.

My favorite entree is a chicken breast in a mustard-cream sauce, a splendid balance of flavors with just a hint of piquancy, and the dish is heightened by the addition of a handful of pickled onions to the sauce.

Although Tony's introduced the giant veal chop as an entree, other St. Louis restaurants have jumped on the dish and made it almost a St. Louis standard. Gian-Peppe's prepares it in a stylish manner, broiled and served with a demi-glaze. An excellent Bordelaise sauce is offered on the side, but the rich, delicious chop tastes fine on its own. Steaks are also top-drawer entrees.

Other chicken dishes have proven first-rate, and lamb chops are satisfactory, if not spectacular.

Standard, well-prepared pastas are superior side dishes, and more of those mussels make an elegant sauce. The wine list is modest but offers some very pleasant accompaniments.

GIAN-TONY'S
5356 Daggett Ave.
(The Hill)
772-4893

❖━❖

Cuisine: Italian
Serves: Dinner, Tuesday–Sunday; lunch, Tuesday–Friday
Prices: Moderate to expensive
Credit Cards: AE, MC, V
Dress: Informal
Reservations: Not accepted on weekends
Handicap Access: Passable
Separate No-Smoking Section: No

One of the many Italian restaurants on the Hill, Gian-Tony's is a small, plain corner location where the meals are simple but extremely well prepared. Nothing is fancy, and not much is new and different, but the plain fare receives loving treatment in the kitchen.

The restaurant is across the street from Berra Park, not named for Yogi but for one of his relatives who was a longtime political power in the city, and I spent several summers on the park's softball diamonds as a star of middle magnitude in over-40 league competitions.

One of the house specialties is the marinara sauce—dark and rich, redolent of tomatoes, capers, garlic, and olives, and splendid atop shrimp, squid, pasta, and other things.

Beef en brochette, the meat lightly dusted with seasoned flour before being broiled with vegetables, is tender and tasty. Tiny bay scallops, sautéd with mushrooms, lemon, and butter, still taste sea-fresh. Veal dishes are generally good.

Tiramisu, light and beautifully soaked in liqueur, is the best of a good crop of desserts. Service can be variable.

GINO'S
4502 Hampton Ave.
351-4187

❖•❖

Cuisine: Italian
Serves: Dinner, Tuesday–Sunday; lunch, Tuesday–Friday
Prices: Inexpensive to moderate
Credit Cards: MC, V
Dress: Casual
Reservations: Not accepted
Handicap Access: Passable
Separate No-Smoking Area: No

Giovanni becomes John when it is translated into English; the natural Italian diminutive is Gino. In the kitchen, however, Mr. Vitale, under any first name, should be referred to as "Sir."

His small storefront restaurant, now two buildings and a patio, sparkles like a well-cut diamond. It is inexpensive and serves huge portions, from pizza to pasta to fancier dishes to dessert (courtesy of his wife, Caterina). I've never had anything less than terrific at Gino's.

Excellent serving personnel snake through the room like great running backs through the opposition defense. And Gino turns out brilliant dishes from a menu that includes a wide range of chicken, veal, and seafood choices; pastas; risottos; and Sicilian specialties like calzone, sausage rolls, and spinach pie.

Calzone is an appetizer the size of a meal; the meat- or cheese-pie is served with ricotta and Parmesan cheese oozing a little around the edges. The crust is light and nicely crisp on the edges. Even toasted ravioli, which I consider a waste of eating time and energy, was quite satisfactory. Salads are good too, with a light, bright vinaigrette dressing atop fresh, crisp greens.

Veal Don Giovanni, a house specialty, involves tasty, tender, high-quality veal sauteed in a wine sauce bolstered by pine nuts and basil. Calamari arrives in a rich marinara sauce, heavy on the tomatoes, and linguine with clam sauce is wondrous. Side orders of pasta with marinara sauce, or just with olive oil and garlic, are beautifully cooked al dente, or just slightly chewy.

Risotto with seafood presents rice with each individual grain standing tall, and mussels, clams, and shrimp are blended perfectly.

Gino's added a wine list since my last visit, and I hope the selection includes plenty of rich, robust reds, which are the perfect accompaniment to his cooking.

Desserts are a match for everything else, with tiramisu displaying a soft, delightful sponge cake and an ample dousing of whipped cream and liqueur. Tarts show a flaky, melt-in-the-mouth crust and are crammed with fruit. And the mascarpone roll, dotted with pistachio nuts, is a richly brilliant blend of textures.

GIOVANNI'S

5201 Shaw Ave. (The Hill) **772-5958**

GIOVANNI'S LITTLE PLACE

14560 Manchester Rd. (West County) **227-7230**

‹—•–•—›

Cuisine: Italian
Serves: Dinner, Monday–Saturday
Prices: Expensive to very expensive
Credit Cards: All major
Dress: Jacket required for men
Reservations: Accepted, advised on weekends
Handicap Access: Satisfactory
Separate No-Smoking Section: No

Giovanni Gabriele, like most of the top-ranked Italian restaurateurs in the city, is an alumnus of Tony's. And like his fellow
alumni, he has set his sights high and worked diligently to place
his own personal stamp on his operation. The elegant Hill establishment is stylish, softly lighted, and expensive but offers outstanding fare with a number of personal touches that make it even
better.

Giovanni's son Frank operates Giovanni's Little Place, a West
County spot of similar menu, slightly less formality, and almost
equal meals.

The pastas at Giovanni's simply sparkle, either as appetizers or
entrees. There's a wide variety of noodles and sauces, and all are
splendid. A large, fish-filled ravioli is rich and tasty; and tortellini,
green or white, are perfectly cooked. Giovanni devised a bow-tie-
shaped noodle in a cream and smoked salmon sauce for one of
Ronald Reagan's inaugurations, and while the dish is delicious, it
may not sit well on Democratic digestions.

I think my favorite (and it's a tough choice) is rigatoni with

128

lobster and vodka sauce. The thick, ridged, pasta stays chewy, and the sauce permeates beautifully.

Other appetizers are outstanding, with a highlight of sautéd squid in a Luciana sauce (similar to a marinara but lighter), as well as a salmon terrine.

Like other restaurants in its class, Giovanni's adds special touches like porcini mushrooms with delicious beef tenderloin in Madeira sauce. The wild mushrooms, only available in certain seasons, are a perfect addition. Scallops sautéd in butter and wine are elegant, and a classic Italian dish like veal piccata, simply prepared in lemon, butter, and wine, is just right.

Beef tenderloin in Bordelaise sauce is elegant, and a red snapper sautéd with artichoke hearts in lemon and wine is outstanding.

Giovanni also found a way to salvage zucchini—slicing it razor-thin and flash-frying until it curled like a potato chip. It is wondrous.

The wine list is strong, with both California and Italian vintages well represented.

A magnificent tiramisu leads the dessert list: the sponge cake of melt-in-the-mouth quality, and the liqueur, whipped cream, and chocolate shavings in perfect amounts. Cannoli is another outstanding dish; the crust is light, crisp, and delicate and the filling is not overly sweet, making the combination as delightful as the meal that preceded it.

GIUSEPPE'S
4141 South Grand Blvd.
(South Side)
832-3779

❖-❖

Cuisine: Italian
Serves: Dinner, Tuesday–Sunday; lunch, Tuesday–Friday
Prices: Moderate to expensive
Credit Cards: AE, MC, V
Dress: Informal
Reservations: Accepted
Handicap Access: Satisfactory
Separate No-Smoking Section: Yes

St. Louisans who like Italian fare are a fortunate group; the city has literally dozens of small restaurants—primarily Sicilian and southern Italian—for highly satisfactory meals at moderate prices.

Among that group, however, Giuseppe's is kind of a first among equals. The south side establishment, which began as a storefront pizza operation and has expanded to include most of the block, offers a wide range of meals in a quality and price ratio that makes it a superior value.

In addition to having the same standard items as most other Italian restaurants, Giuseppe's prepares some that few seem willing to attempt, like chicken livers. I admit a weakness for them, regardless of cooking style. Giuseppe's dusts them with seasoned flour, then sautés them with onions cooked until they're almost caramelized, and the result is a delight. They're great on top of pasta, too.

Green bell peppers sautéd in olive oil make for a dazzling appetizer, with the peppers softened and slightly sweetened by the cooking process. Spectacular!

Unfortunately, there's toasted ravioli, too, no different from that

130

served at most other restaurants. I just don't see the dish's appeal, though I know it's popular.

Homemade sausage, spiced with fennel for a fascinatingly different flavor, is outstanding and served baked, broiled, or fried, with or without spaghetti on the side.

Veal pizziola, with a rich tomato sauce sparked with green olives and heavy with garlic, is splendid, and pasta dishes are exemplary, under a wide range of both red and white sauces.

The wine list is shorter on Italian selections than it might be, but there are some pleasant California choices at reasonable prices. Desserts are standard.

GUIDRY'S CAJUN RESTAURANT
8100 Ivory St.
(Far South)
631-3646

❖❖❖

Cuisine: Cajun
Serves: Dinner, Monday–Saturday; lunch, Monday–Friday
Prices: Inexpensive to moderate
Credit Cards: All major
Dress: Casual
Reservations: Not accepted
Handicap Access: Difficult (steps at entrance)
Separate No-Smoking Area: No

Of all the restaurants discussed in this book, Guidry's is the most difficult to find on a St. Louis map, mainly because Ivory Avenue is a very short street in the far southeast corner of the city. To find it, take I-55 south to Germania, turn left on Germania to Alabama, and then turn left again. Ivory is close by, and Guidry's is in a plain, white frame building on a corner.

Giant manufacturing plants loom across the street, trains rumble by from time to time, and through the smoke and steam, it's slightly reminiscent of Kenner, across the Mississippi River from New Orleans.

Guidry's also does not have a liquor license, so bring your own wine and beer. If you forget, there's another New Orleans look-alike nearby, a combination liquor store and bait shop.

I think Guidry's is worth the trip; I'm very fond of spicy Cajun cooking, and Guidry's sometimes pushes the spicing to the limit. Service is relaxed and not always efficient, but the atmosphere is so laid-back that it doesn't seem important.

The menu is Cajun and Creole but also includes chicken wings for grown-ups. The menu says "spicy," and you can take that to the bank.

Gumbo is described as the house specialty, and it is splendid, sometimes with chicken and sausage—sometimes with shrimp and sausage, always with lots of okra and file (ground sassafras) to add body and flavor, served over well-cooked rice, with deep-fried corn bread (better known as hush puppies) served alongside.

Boudin sausage, with rice inside the casing, is tasty, and so are steamed crawfish, available in season. Seasonal seafood specialties show up on the menu from time to time, and some softshell crabs that arrived just in time for my dinner were spectacular.

Red beans and rice are good but tend to be overcooked and mushy, more like Mexican refried beans. Jambalaya, with chicken, rice, and the spicy Cajun ham called tasso, is a lovely blend of flavors; and shrimp étouffée, blending shrimp and vegetables over rice, is delicious.

Beignets, those sugared holeless doughnuts, and chicory coffee take care of dessert cravings.

My own wine choices tend to those that are off-dry, or slightly sweet, like a gewurztraminer or a riesling, or even a rosé or—perish the thought—a white zinfandel. Something about the sweetness seems to cut through the spice, just as it does with spicy Chinese food.

HUNAN CAFE
2615 Hampton Ave.
645-2026

Cuisine: Chinese
Serves: Dinner, every day; lunch, Monday–Friday
Prices: Inexpensive to moderate
Credit Cards: AE, MC, V
Dress: Casual
Reservations: Accepted
Handicap Access: Satisfactory
Separate No-Smoking Section: No

For a few bright years, Chinese restaurants, with the cuisine of Szechuan and Hunan, were opening regularly in the St. Louis area, each bringing a new touch and, perhaps, different dishes. Then everything leveled off. Too many of them seemed to be copying from one another. Menus appeared to be identical. And the city still lacks a truly elegant Chinese restaurant.

This is not to knock the Hunan Cafe, but just to point out a local problem. The Hunan Cafe has pleasing meals at pleasing prices, but it lacks the imaginative touches that might make it exceptional.

There are good pot-stickers, or dumplings, and the hot-and-sour soup is pleasant, if not spicy-hot enough. Egg rolls are passable; crab Rangoon is pretty good.

Entrees are also standard, with Kung Pao squid showing evidence of lots of peppers. General Tso's chicken, with red peppers and peanuts, also has considerable style. Shrimp in the traditonal Cantonese lobster sauce is satisfactory.

THE KING AND I
3157 South Grand Blvd.
(South Side)
771-1777

❖❖

Cuisine: Thai
Serves: Lunch and dinner, Tuesday–Sunday
Prices: Inexpensive to moderate
Credit Cards: All major
Dress: Casual
Reservations: Accepted
Handicap Access: Satisfactory
Separate No-Smoking Section: Yes

The area's first Thai restaurant moved a few blocks to larger and more comfortable quarters last autumn and, at the same time, solidified its reputation as the area's best. Service is a little erratic, and there are sometimes language problems, but meals are good enough that minor problems can be ignored.

The cuisine can be fiery, but it also can be extremely delicate. The use of spicing can be geared to the diner's preference, and as in most good Thai operations, they use more than mere pepper. Ginger, garlic, coconut milk, lemongrass, coriander, cumin, and other herbs and spices are all part of Thai cooking. In terms of temperature, there are cool dishes as well as hot ones, and many of the cool ones are mighty spicy.

To confuse things even more, let's begin with egg rolls, which are cool, but not very spicy, and not at all like Chinese egg rolls. They are wrapped in a skin of rice flour, like a crêpe, and filled with bean curd, sprouts, cucumbers, scrambled egg, and other things. The spicing is delicate, but a sauce comes alongside to build any necessary fire.

Spring rolls are similar to Chinese egg rolls, but thinner.

135

Bangkok toasts are bread quarters topped with an egg–green-onion–ground-pork mixture, then deep fried and served with a tangy sauce—slightly greasy, very delicious.

Bangkok wings are a tasty, unusual appetizer, starting with the fat part of a chicken wing, stuffed with ground shrimp, pork, and spices, then battered and fried. A tempura appetizer plate brought shrimp, onion rings, and green pepper strips deep-fried in a batter similar to that used in Japanese cooking.

The King and I offers two different styles of curry, one dry and one soupy, at varying heat intensities. Green tends to be hotter than red, but again, the spicing can be ordered mild, medium, or hot, and the kitchen responds well.

Pork and Napa cabbage was delicious, and chicken, in soup with coconut milk and lemon grass, showed a tangy, almost sweet-hot flavor.

Grapao shrimp, with red peppers (watch out for them), green peppers, and a tangy sauce, is splendid. Pad Ped squid, pleasingly tender and stir-fried with garlic and chili peppers—lots and lots of chili peppers—is extremely fiery and delicious. There are also noodle dishes and vegetarian dishes of all types, and all are excellent.

I like beer with Oriental food, and Singha, imported from Thailand, is a good accompaniment. Sake is available too.

LoRUSSO'S

3121 Watson Rd. **647-6222**

TUTTO BENE

12153 Manchester Rd. **965-8200**

Cuisine: Italian
Serves: Dinner, every night; lunch, Monday–Friday
Prices: Moderate to expensive
Credit Cards: All major
Dress: Informal
Reservations: Only for parties of six or more, Monday–Thursday, at Watson Road; no restrictions on Manchester Road
Handicap Access: Satisfactory
Separate No-Smoking Section: Yes

One of the major restaurant success stories of recent years is LoRusso's. Originally a 28-seat storefront, with Rich LoRusso in the kitchen, brother Tom out front, and their mother bringing desserts from home, it expanded first to a busy, open-kitchen establishment not far from home, then to a second site, Tutto Bene, in the West County.

I prefer the Watson Road location, though there are similar dishes at both places. The emphasis seems to be on pasta and pizza on Manchester and the preparation shows less imagination and style.

LoRusso's menu is classic Italian, but a lot of love and a calm hand with herbs and spices adds some piquant touches here and there. Marsala sauce—used on beef, chicken, or veal, is superior, especially with rich, tasty, well-grilled beef. Garlicky marinara sauce, bursting with capers and black olives, is elegant atop calamari; it was also outstanding one night with a tasty, perfectly grilled grouper. Gorgonzola cheese adds a tangy contrast to a

137

edges, were ideal under the lightest of wine sauces, allowing the full scallop flavor to come dancing through.

Fried or sautéd calamari is a tasty appetizer, as is anchovy toast. I'm glad to see the hairy little fish making a comeback on St. Louis menus; for a while they were difficult to find as pizza toppings, and I missed them. Minestrone soup, with a hearty beef stock, is thick and rich, the veteran of a long term in the stockpot.

Farfalle, or bow-tie noodles, are light and tasty with fresh salmon in the sauce, and the traditional tortellini with prosciutto, mushrooms, and green peas is just right.

Tutto Bene makes a lot of cheeseless pizzas, topped with pesto, or sun-dried tomatoes, or grilled eggplant, or roasted garlic, and they're tasty. The pasta list is lengthy and a puttanesca sauce, with garlic, anchovies, red peppers, and tomatoes, is a highly spiced delight.

Mama LoRusso still prepares the rich, wonderful cassata cake, and her cheesecakes are outstanding too. Tom does the tiramisu, with lady fingers, mascarpone cheese, espresso, and other taste sensations culminating in a rich, delicious pastry.

O'CONNELL'S PUB
4958 Shaw Ave.
(At Kingshighway)
773-6600

◆━◆

Cuisine: Hamburgers, other bar fare
Serves: Lunch and dinner, Monday–Saturday (same menu)
Prices: Inexpensive
Credit Cards: MC, V
Dress: Casual
Reservations: Not accepted
Handicap Access: Satisfactory
Separate No-Smoking Section: No

For me, and for thousands like me, the search for a hamburger ends right here, in a wood-paneled bar and restaurant that has become a St. Louis classic. The giant 9- to 10-ounce burgers, of fresh, unfrozen beef, grilled to order and served on a toasted sesame-seed bun with pickle and raw onion on the side, are arguably the best in the nation.

The other choices, like roast beef, Italian sausage, and peppers, and daily specials (fish and chips on Fridays, rib tips on Saturdays) achieve the very highest level of bar food. Soups are good, chili is satisfactory, french fries are thin, crisp, and freshly cooked in clean oil.

O'Connell's was the final flickering ember of Gaslight Square, and when Jack Parker moved it to the Near South Side, at the edge of the Hill, in 1972, his customers mourned. The newspaper reporters, leftover hippies, and drinkers who had called it home railed that Parker had ruined everything by moving to a more accessible location. It would be different, and no one would go there, said the prophets of gloom and doom.

Well, the prophets were wrong, and so was I.

The regulars were promptly joined by most of the western world, and O'Connell's is patronized by the entire range of St. Louisans and out-of-towners, including a Japanese television crew in search of a typical American restaurant. Coats and ties share space with rowdy T-shirts for sandwiches and imported beer and ale. The evening crowd is younger and can be more raucous, but it remains mostly well mannered. Parker stopped cooking some years ago and now devotes most of his time to a successful antique business upstairs.

O'Connell's is for eating, drinking, and talking: no jukebox, no video games, no television, no piano. Classical music is played on cassettes, but not so loud as to interfere with conversation.

The pictures of Irish patriots and literary figures on the walls are not always who they seem, but they add a nice touch to one of the great bar-restaurants of my experience. The waitresses are not only friendly and as quick as fireflies, but they're individuals, led by the lovely, soft-spoken Nora, who has been there since the Gaslight Square days. So have several bartenders, providing a wonderful sense of history and continuity. Add the superior food and the result is something truly outstanding.

OLYMPIA KEBOB HOUSE AND TAVERNA
1543 McCausland Ave.
781-1299

❖❖❖

Cuisine: Greek
Serves: Dinner, every day; lunch, Monday–Saturday
Prices: Inexpensive to moderate
Credit Cards: All major
Dress: Casual
Reservations: Accepted
Handicap Access: Passable
Separate No-Smoking Section: No

Noisy and cheerful, with some of the friendliest staff in the area, the Olympia is an inexpensive gathering spot with outstanding, modestly priced Grecian fare, and when Grandma is on hand, pastries and desserts that are matchless.

Daily specials bolster standards like gyro sandwiches, moussaka, pasticcio (or pastitsio) and the like, and items like stuffed peppers, stuffed eggplant, and dolmathes (stuffed grape leaves) show up often. Dolmathes, in a rich lemon sauce, are exciting, and as an eggplant lover, I can swear by the stuffed variety.

Pasticcio, a smooth, flavorful macaroni-beef-cheese casserole, is accented with a touch of nutmeg. A plate of feta cheese, sprinkled with olive oil and oregano, plus some dark olives, is a delightful accompaniment to a predinner drink. Another winning appetizer is taramosalata, or salmon roe blended with lemon juice and olive oil for a superior dip.

Baklava is available, but Grandma's kourambeathes, Greek wedding cookies topped with powdered sugar, or her Galaktobureko—philo dough, chopped nuts, and honey—are great. Those desserts help make the aura at the Olympia so joyous that at any moment I expect to see Anthony Quinn and Melina Mercouri start to dance.

PAT'S BAR & GRILL
6400 Oakland Ave.
(South Side of Forest Park)
647-6553

Cuisine: American bar food
Serves: Lunch and dinner, Monday–Saturday (same menu)
Prices: Inexpensive
Credit Cards: MC, V
Dress: Casual
Reservations: Not applicable
Handicap Access: Satisfactory (narrow aisles a problem)
Separate No-Smoking Section: No

Pat's is the sort of place that is familiarly known as a "neighborhood institution," except that its location across the street from Forest Park and the Zoo, and only a short walk from the Arena, gives it a citywide clientele of softball players, hockey fans, concert-goers, and others who either play for fun or pay for tickets.

The neighborhood is known as Dogtown, a term left over from the 1904 World's Fair, and Pat's provides some of the best traditional St. Louis bar food in town—items like fried chicken, catfish, chicken livers, gizzards, and that south St. Louis institution, brain sandwiches.

I admit that the brain sandwich is one of the foods I simply can't handle, but those who like the particular dish speak highly of the preparation here.

I know that the fried chicken livers are outstanding, usually juicy and crisp, with an excellent batter, and both fried chicken and fried catfish are exemplary. Pat's also does wonderful chicken wings, without the hot sauce but with splendid flavor of their own. Hamburgers are good, if not great, and fried onion rings are better than average.

The noise level tends to be high, especially after softball games.

143

PHO GRAND
3191 South Grand Blvd.
664-7435

━━━

Cuisine: Vietnamese
Serves: Lunch and dinner, every day except Tuesday
Prices: Inexpensive to moderate
Credit Cards: None
Dress: Casual
Reservations: Not applicable
Handicap Access: Satisfactory
Separate No-Smoking Section: No

One of the first Vietnamese restaurants on South Grand Boulevard, an area that now has a number of Southeast Asian dining and grocery establishments, Pho Grand serves light, delicately flavored cuisine, often atop noodles or in soup.

There is considerable use of garlic and onions, a tang of pepper now and then, and much lemongrass, cilantro, and ginger, applied to bring heightened flavors, but not overpowering ones.

A variety of rolled items, served cold, make excellent appetizers. Egg rolls involve chopped vegetables and shredded pork in lettuce. Spring and summer rolls are wrapped in rice-flour crêpes (for lack of a better word), with the former including vegetables, shrimp, and pork, the latter eliminating the shrimp.

Crushed rice, a little like sticky rice, is a fine base for chicken with ginger and onions, or for the slightly spicier chicken with chili and lemon grass. Egg noodles or translucent vermicelli noodles work well in a number of dishes, starting with charcoal-broiled or barbecued pork and a variety of seafood items. I liked rice noodle soup with meatballs, though the texture of the meatballs is softer and the meat more finely ground than in, say, Italian meatballs.

144

Service is friendly, though there are occasional language barriers.

Homemade lemonade is a summer treat, and beers from Asia go nicely with the Pho Grand cuisine.

Then there's the wonderful Vietnamese coffee that shows the French influence on this Asian nation. It's black and strong, served in what looks like French "cafe filtre," and drips slowly into the glass which contains some condensed milk waiting patiently. When enough hot coffee is in the glass, ice cubes are added and the whole thing is busily stirred. The result is sweet, strong, and delicious, and one of my favorite beverages.

SAM'S ST. LOUIS STEAKHOUSE
10205 Gravois Road
(At Laclede Station Road)
849-3033

Cuisine: Classic American steaks and chops
Serves: Dinner, Monday–Saturday
Prices: Moderate to expensive
Credit Cards: All major
Reservations: Accepted
Handicap Access: Satisfactory
Separate No-Smoking Section: Yes

If keeping it simple is the way to restaurant success, then Sam's St. Louis Steakhouse has found the magic marker. Opened in the late summer of 1991, Sam's is a spin-off of Andria's, in Fairview Heights, Illinois, but has several major advantages: It takes reservations, it doesn't have a salad bar, and it has sufficient space between tables.

Sam's is your basic steak-and-chop house, with prime rib, too, and a grilled chicken breast, all of immense size. Dinner is a salad, meat, a vegetable, and a giant baked potato. There's a soup of the day, but no other appetizer. You can also get fried zucchini or french-fried potatoes, but that's it.

Sirloin, filet mignon, and prime rib come in two sizes—immense and stupendous—which provides Sam's with a nifty gimmick: Order either sirloin or prime rib or the large filet, add $7, and get one steak plus two potatoes, two salads and two vegetables. Then divide the meat for yourself and your companion. Voilà! Dinner for two.

Bean soup makes a good introduction to dinner, and though the salads are mostly iceberg lettuce, they're fresh and crisp, with homemade croutons and tasty dressings.

The meat was exemplary: perfectly cooked, flavorful, and practically fork-tender. The rib had been charred on the outside (Sam's calls it "French style") and was delightfully tender in the middle. The steaks, blackened a little on the edges, still red or pink in the middle, were extremely juicy and flavorful. The pork chop was as good as any I've ever had, and cooking double-thick pork chops is tricky. They have to be cooked through, yet overcooking makes the meat tough and stringy. These were perfect.

The baked potato, blessedly foilless, was rich and mealy, and hot enough not to acquire a fatal chill from sour cream and butter. Even the zucchini was a pleasant surprise, with the vegetable remaining sweet and juicy under a nice batter.

Service is crisp and efficient, from an experienced staff, and while the wine list is limited, one can find a hearty red or two to accompany the beef. Desserts have been second-rate, but after dinner at Sam's, one doesn't need dessert. Believe me.

SLIDER'S
5127 Hampton Ave.
752-7126

❖⬥

Cuisine: Seafood
Serves: Dinner, every day; lunch, Monday–Friday
Prices: Moderate
Credit Cards: All major
Dress: Informal
Reservations: Accepted only for parties of six or more
Handicap Access: Satisfactory
Separate No-Smoking Area: No

As fresh seafood became more and more available through the 1980s, more and more St. Louis restaurants began to specialize. Prices came down through the law of supply and demand, and restaurants of moderate price range, like Slider's, began serving the products of ocean, river, and lake, both the shelled and the finned variety.

Slider's, part of the restaurant strip along the southern stretch of Hampton Avenue, was opened by some transplanted Floridians, who generally know how to prepare and serve seafood.

The small restaurant, of modest decor and rather bright lighting, has a good selection, including that Florida favorite, grouper, either grilled or baked after being rolled in bread crumbs and a few pecans. Grouper is rich and hearty, too much so for those who say, "I love fish, but I don't like it when it tastes fishy," but those are people who should be in steak houses.

Salmon is excellent, and so are New Orleans dishes like crawfish étouffée. Sautéd shrimp and scallops are also properly, and simply, prepared, with a little butter, a good amount of garlic, a heavy squirt of lemon, and maybe a little white wine.

Appetizers include a roll of pastry dough stuffed with crabmeat,

148

a very good baked crab dip, clams casino, and a few others. Salads are ordinary, but the Key lime pie is superior, with that delicate, light-yellow color that identifies real Key limes, and a pleasing tartness that is the perfect touch after a big meal.

SPIRO'S

3122 Watson Rd. (South) **645-8383**

8406 Natural Bridge Rd. (Mid-County) **382-8074**

1054 N. Woods Mill Rd. (West County) **878-4449**

13134 Tesson Ferry Rd. (South County) **843-7161**

Cuisine: Greek

Serves: Dinner, Monday–Saturday; lunch, Monday–Friday; hours and details may vary at different locations

Prices: Moderate to expensive

Credit Cards: All major

Dress: Informal

Reservations: Accepted, advised on weekends

Handicap Access: Satisfactory

Separate No-Smoking Section: No

The Spiro's story is one of the great American tales, the climb-to-success saga that we all learned about in our history books, but which seems to occur so rarely today.

Larry Karagiannis is one of a large family of Greeks who worked in the restaurant and hotel business. They were cooks, maitre d's, waiters, and dozens of them served me in one capacity or another through the years, at restaurants of every style.

Larry graduated from the University of Missouri–St. Louis with a degree in history but could not find a teaching job. With family help, he opened the first Spiro's, on Natural Bridge Road near the campus, serving mainly lunches of good and familiar Greek meals—stuffed grape leaves, egg-lemon soup, shish kebab, moussaka, pastichio, baklava.

Success there led to three other restaurants, but Watson Road is the flagship. I've had good meals at the others, but not quite as good as at Watson Road, where Larry is in charge and where—if

150

the conditions are right—he will make the finest steak tartar in the area, using only a French chef's knife and considerable skill.

It isn't on the menu, but I happened to see him making it one night and, on a subsequent visit, asked for it. He provided with the same proud smile as any craftsman asked to share his wares.

He begins with a chunk of beef tenderloin similar to that used in many restaurants, but once it's in front of him, he goes to work with his knife, and the difference between chopped and ground beef in a steak tartar must be tasted to be understood. Once chopped to his satisfaction, he adds the other traditional ingredients of onion, garlic, a couple of anchovies, a raw egg, and some spices. Freshness makes a difference, too, and it's an exemplary dish.

Spiro's menu includes all the traditional Greek dishes, beginning with saganaki, or fried kasseri cheese topped with brandy and flamed at tableside. Dolmathes, grape leaves stuffed with rice-studded ground beef, are nicely spiced and very tasty, and the egg-lemon soup also is first-rate.

Casserole dishes like moussaka (ground beef, eggplant, and potatoes) and pastichio (ground beef, macaroni, and cheeses) are superior, and traditional shish kebab, of either beef or lamb, brings delicious meat, delightfully marinated. Lamb chops are satisfactory, fried smelts can be delicious, and lamb liver and sweetbreads are excellent.

Vegetables tend to be overdone, and there's a barely adequate wine list, but it includes the wonderful Greek rosé called Roditis. Delicious, rich, supersweet baklava is always right for dessert, especially with dark, thick coffee.

UNCLE BILL'S PANCAKE HOUSE
3427 South Kingshighway
(South Side)
832-1973

❖❖

Cuisine: General American
Serves: 24 hours (except 3 p.m. Sunday to 6 a.m. Monday)
Prices: Inexpensive to moderate
Credit Cards: Not accepted
Dress: Casual
Reservations: Not applicable
Handicap Access: Satisfactory
Separate No-Smoking Section: Yes

Poet Thomas Gray wrote about the plowman who "slowly wends his weary way." Well, late-night wanderers do the same thing, and to them, Uncle Bill's Pancake House shows a welcome light. The South Side spot is a St. Louis tradition, and its 24-hour presence was a welcome sight for generations of homeward-bound folks. (See above for a minor change in hours.)

Pancakes, waffles, eggs, and other breakfast items are well prepared and fresh, and the coffee cup stays full, too, an important consideration at breakfast time.

There are lunches and dinners, with good fried chicken and simple fare, but I just don't seem to identify with Uncle Bill except at breakfast.

MID-COUNTY

West of the city limits and east of Lindbergh Boulevard, covering communities like Brentwood, Clayton, Ladue, Maplewood, Richmond Heights, Rock Hill, Warson Woods, Webster Groves, and University City.

Al Baker's (Clayton)
L'Auberge Bretonne (Clayton)
Bar Jamaica Jerk Pit (University City)
Bernard's (Clayton)
Blueberry Hill (University City)
Brandt's Market and Cafe (University City)
Busch's Grove (Ladue)
Cafe Manhattan (Clayton)
Cafe Napoli (Clayton)
Cafe Zoe (Clayton)
Candicci's (Clayton)
Cardwell's (Clayton)
Carl's Drive-In (Rock Hill)
Casa Gallardo Grill (Richmond Heights)
Charcoal House (Rock Hill)
Chez Louis (Clayton)
Cousin Hugo's (Maplewood)
Cyrano's (Richmond Heights)
The Dining Room and The Grill
European Caffe' (Richmond Heights)
Fio's La Fourchette (Richmond Heights)
Girarrosto (Clayton)
Hacienda (Rock Hill)
Hsu's Chinese Restaurant (Olivette)
Hunan Wok (Brentwood)

Joe & Charlie's (Richmond Heights)
Ken Barry's Restaurant & Lounge (University City)
King Doh (Warson Woods)
Koh-i-Noor (University City)
Mai Lee (University City)
The Mandarin House (Overland)
Max's Bar & Grill (Clayton)
Miss Hulling's Cafeteria (Webster Groves; see Downtown listings)
Nobu's Japanese City(University City)
La Patisserie/Cafe Jules (University City)
The Red Sea (University City)
Riddle's Penultimate Cafe (University City)
Royal Chinese B.B.Q. (University City)
Sadie Thompson's (Clayton)
Saleem's (University City, Chesterfield)
Seki's Japanese Restaurant (University City)
Ted & Teiko's (Warson Woods)
Thai Cafe (University City)
Webster Grill & Cafe (Webster Groves)
The Wishing Well (Berkeley)
Zinnia (Webster Groves)
Zorba's (Clayton, University City, Webster Groves)

AL BAKER'S
8101 Clayton Rd.
(Clayton)
863-8878

❖❖

Cuisine: American with Italian and French overtones
Serves: Dinner, Monday–Saturday
Prices: Expensive to very expensive
Credit Cards: All major
Dress: Jacket required in main dining room
Reservations: Accepted and advised
Handicap Access: Satisfactory
Separate No-Smoking Section: Yes

Decorated in the Diamond Jim Brady tradition, with lots of dark wood and red trim, Al Baker's long was known for vest-popping dining featuring giant steaks, rich sauces, and heavy meals. In recent years, it has changed a little, with no loss of excellence. The elegant steaks are still there, but sauces are lighter, the fish selection has grown by leaps and bounds, and the restaurant now represents the entire dining spectrum.

Located in the heart of the Mid-County area, convenient to just about anywhere, Baker's traditionally has been a place to see and be seen, with an active bar and a sumptuous dining room. Athletes, politicians, major wheeler-dealers, and others fill the large chairs and enjoy what probably is the area's largest wine list, with a fine stock of great vintages.

As starters, oysters, either on the half shell or baked in their own juice, are always good, and clams Casino are commendable. Stone crabs come by air from Miami; they're costly and, unfortunately, they don't display the flavor they show at home. A shipment from Texas showed similar problems on a recent visit.

Salads, tossed tableside, show a good selection of greens and a light, pleasing oil-and-vinegar dressing bolstered with a strong hint of anchovy.

Steaks and chops have been the heart of Baker's cuisine, and a longtime Baker specialty is "hobo steak": thick slices of filet mignon sautéd tableside with a Bordelaise sauce heightened by tangy mustard. It's a splendid treatment of a fine cut of beef.

Broiled fish comes out of the kitchen at the perfect moment, cooked to the proper point, and often so good it needs nothing but a squirt of lemon. Veal marsala shows a nice Italian hand, and the Greek-style lamb is tender and redolent with rosemary.

Pasta makes a good side dish, but even better are Baker's Italian-fried potatoes, cooked crisp in olive oil with a dash of green onions. Speaking of Italian, one of the best dishes at Baker's is the sautéd sweet sausage, accompanied by a lovely, delicious mess— that's the only word for it—of onions and bell peppers. It's an old-fashioned dish, but oh boy! is it ever good.

Chocolate mousse is a common dessert, but it arrives here as an uncommonly good way to end a meal.

L'AUBERGE BRETONNE
200 South Brentwood Blvd.
(Clayton)
721-0100

Cuisine: French (American at lunch)
Serves: Dinner, Monday–Saturday; lunch, Monday–Friday
Prices: Expensive to very expensive
Credit Cards: All major
Dress: Informal (jackets preferred)
Reservations: Accepted
Handicap Access: Satisfactory
Separate No-Smoking Section: Yes

When one realizes that French cuisine has been the world's standard since Catherine de Medici brought the basics from Italy during the Renaissance, one wonders why it took so long to make the journey to St. Louis.

Thanks are thus due to Jean-Claude Guillossou, who could be called the godfather of French cuisine in St. Louis. He began as the chef at a local country club, then opened the first L'Auberge Bretonne in a West County strip shopping center in 1976. Two moves later, he is in Clayton, across the street from Shaw Park, in a site that was home to the Coal Hole for many years.

Guillossou, with the commitment to pragmatism shown by his countrymen, has retained the Coal Hole's popular lunch menu, though he smiles when he notes that "perhaps we have improved a few of the dishes here and there." Dinner is when his Breton heritage comes to the fore. Through the years, his success and that of his brother-in-law, Marcel Keraval, at Cafe de France, downtown, led the way for a number of French restaurants, and the entire area has benefited from the efforts of these two men and their wives, who are sisters.

L'Auberge Bretonne has a stylish dining room and superior service, with a menu that blends nouvelle and haute cuisine in excellent style, and dinner is always a pleasure. Like most fine chefs, Guillossou uses the produce and the meats of the season, matched nicely with seasonings and sauces. Fresh herbs are in plentiful supply, and there's a nice, but not cute, use of fruit.

The appetizer list is led by some wonderful pâtés, both smooth and coarse, and a duck liver offering is rich and delicately flavored. Pork and veal are slightly stronger, often with nuts in the mixture, and they're outstanding. Quenelles of pike are elegant, and so are raviolis stuffed with mussels. When the crayfish bisque is on the menu, don't pass it by.

Salads show excellent, homemade dressing, and the Caesar salad is exceptional. Entrees run the range of French cuisine with overtones of the chef's native Brittany in the use of apples and their alcoholic by-product, Calvados. Roast duck is always a delight, with part of the fowl in a pastry crust, part simply sliced. The flavor is rich and delicate, and no matter what fruit is used as a base for the sauce, it is a perfect complement to the duck itself.

Fresh fish is a regular, and delicious, part of the menu, from salmon that is broiled and served with a simple sauce, to a seafood sausage that blends crab meat, shrimp, scallops, and garlic in a delightful garlicky mixture. Quail, stuffed with veal mousse and wild rice, is succulent.

Desserts and cheeses are elegant, with pastries and sorbets that are French, rich, and delicious.

BAR JAMAICA JERK PIT
7828 Olive Street Rd.
(University City)
725-5156

❖❖❖

Cuisine: Jamaican, Caribbean
Serves: Dinner, every day; lunch, Monday–Saturday
Prices: Inexpensive to moderate
Credit Cards: All major
Dress: Casual
Reservations: Accepted
Handicap Access: Satisfactory
Separate No-Smoking Section: No

Any search in St. Louis for the spicy, delicious foods of the Caribbean begins and ends here, where Albertine Thompson runs the only place in town and where bottles of the city's finest selection of hot sauces are the main table decoration.

"Jerk" or "jerked" refers to the Jamaican term for barbecued or grilled meats and fish, usually marinated before cooking and served with a spicy sauce. Spicy starts high on the fire scale, and bottles on the tables range in temperature from very hot to *oh, my goodness!* Be careful.

Jamaican beef patties are filled with spicy meat in a crisp dough that is itself lightly spiced, and they're an ideal beginning with a bottle of Jamaica-brewed Red Stripe beer. The patty also is made with a vegetable filling.

Beef, pork, chicken, fish, and goat are all on the menu, some in a light, tasty curry sauce, others "roti," which involves strips or chunks of meat, or curried vegetables, in a flat bread similar to pita. Entrees include sweet and sour fish or chicken, smoked meats and fish cooked in the "jerk pit," stews, and several vegetarian dishes. Most are accompanied by roast corn on the cob or the traditional Jamaican rice and peas.

Mrs. Thompson also makes the desserts, including a delightful rum cake and several fruit dishes, some with a variety of liqueurs or rum for flavor and zest. Service can be a little slow, but it's always friendly, and it gives dinner at the Bar Jamaica a nice feeling.

BERNARD'S
26 North Meramec Ave.
(Clayton)
727-7004

❖❖

Cuisine: French Bistro
Serves: Breakfast, lunch, and dinner every day
Prices: Moderate
Credit Cards: All major
Dress: Informal
Reservations: Not accepted
Handicap Access: Satisfactory
Separate No-Smoking Section: Yes

The most charming hotel coffee shop in the area, Bernard's got that role almost by accident. It was opened as a bistro/brasserie complement to the more expensive and fancier Chez Louis, just across the hall in the same building.

When the building was remodeled and the elegant Seven Gables Inn opened with Chez Louis as the dining room, Bernard's became the hotel coffee shop.

With lovely art-exhibit posters on the walls, this is a charming little spot with excellent food and a bar with a superior list of wines by the glass.

Fine French and sourdough bread serve as the base for some splendid sandwiches, like the classic "croque monsieur," or grilled ham and cheese, and the soups are outstanding. Chicken salad is superior, and so are the grilled sausages. A few dinner entrees, like fresh fish or grilled chicken, join the menu later in the day, and desserts are terrific.

160

BLUEBERRY HILL
6504 Delmar Blvd.
(University City)
727-0880

❖❖

Cuisine: American bar food
Serves: Lunch and dinner, every day (same menu); Sunday brunch
Prices: Inexpensive
Credit Cards: AE, MC, V
Dress: Casual
Reservations: Only for large parties
Handicap Access: Satisfactory
Separate No-Smoking Section: Yes

Like Topsy, Blueberry Hill "just growed," from one storefront to most of a block, from one impressive jukebox to a collection of boxes, sheet music, Elvis memorabilia, and the sort of stuff that gave the Smithsonian its start.

Joe and Linda Edwards hung on through the University City Loop's bad times and are among the leaders of the revival of a neighborhood to one of the city's best browsing, dining, drinking, and listening areas, complete with stars in the sidewalk to honor St. Louis' best.

Along with things to look at, there are things to do here, too—darts, pinball, dominoes, checkers, Monopoly, Clue, and other games on boards laminated into the table tops.

The recently remodeled and enlarged kitchen hasn't improved the food a lot but has made service faster. The burgers, soups, sandwiches, chili, and other bar food are of good quality, and there are dozens of different beers, along with imported hard cider on draft, to wash them down.

Seasonal window displays, courtesy of Linda, and Rock 'n' Roll

161

Beer, courtesy of Joe (but rockin' awful stuff) are additional high-lights.

BRANDT'S MARKET AND CAFE
6525 Delmar Blvd.
(University City)
727-3663

❖-❖

Cuisine: Eclectic
Serves: Breakfast, lunch, and dinner, every day (to 5 p.m. Sundays)
Prices: Inexpensive to moderate
Credit Cards: All major
Dress: Informal
Reservations: Not applicable
Handicap Access: Entrance satisfactory, rest rooms extremely difficult (narrow aisles)
Separate No-Smoking Section: No smoking in restaurant

When I moved to St. Louis in 1955, I lived in the University City Loop—a jolly neighborhood with several restaurants, a good bookstore, other necessary service establishments, movie houses, and Brandt's, a good liquor store with a fair wine selection.

In subsequent years, the neighborhood deteriorated, then was reborn stronger than ever. Today the five or six blocks of Delmar Boulevard from Skinker to Kingsland (how many blocks depends on which side of Delmar you're walking) is home to the widest selection of ethnic cuisine in the area. There are more bookstores, lots of boutiques, the same vital services—and Brandt's Cafe, where Jay Brandt operates one of the area's most unusual places to dine, on the site of his father's liquor store.

Brandt's also is a fine wine store and a gourmet grocery, and in truth, it's both more and less than a restaurant. It's more of a wonderful snack shop, with all sorts of delicacies coming out of a tiny kitchen, from breakfast through dinner. There's sidewalk seating and live music on weekends, and it offers a splendidly convivial ambiance at any time of the day or evening, for anything from fancy coffees and teas to superior food items.

The menu, on a chalkboard, varies daily, though there's always an omelet chef on hand for Sunday brunch. Food is ordered from a counter with eye-catching items on display, and when it's ready, you pick it up and carry it to your table.

There are fresh, wonderful muffins and pastries of all types in the mornings, and splendid breads throughout the day. Two young women who became a business called Pandora used to bake on the premises, grew successful enough to open their own bakery, and still provide goodies to Brandt's, and to other restaurants throughout the area.

Espressos, cappuccinos, Vietnamese drip coffee with condensed milk, and other coffee and tea pleasures are on hand, along with a superior collection of domestic and imported beer and a wide range of fruit juices. Many dishes are made with health-bringing ingredients—or at least with ingredients that won't harm you—and there's a wide array of salads that can make vegetarianism a pleasure.

Blini, those small Russian buckwheat pancakes, are splendid, especially with smoked salmon, and Brandt's chicken salad, with almonds and curry, is a delight. So is the classic Provençal salade niçoise. Soups and black bean chili are excellent, and fresh quiche in a flaky crust, or a potato-cheese tart, are sure winners.

Sandwiches are built imaginatively, on pita or the Middle Eastern flatbread called lavosh, or on black-as-night pumpernickel, whole-grain breads, or even bagels.

Desserts run the gamut, and there's ice cream, too.

In other words, you can build a meal that will be light or heavy, health-enhancing or totally hedonistic.

The choice—as it should be—is yours.

164

BUSCH'S GROVE
9180 Clayton Rd.
(Ladue)
993-0011

Cuisine: American
Serves: Lunch and dinner, Tuesday–Saturday
Prices: Expensive
Credit Cards: MC, V
Dress: Informal
Reservations: Accepted
Handicap Access: Satisfactory
Separate No-Smoking Section: Yes

Busch's Grove has been in its Mid-County location so long that it has seen almost a 180-degree shift in terms of where its ever-loyal clientele lived. Once upon a time, it was at the western edge of what was considered to be civilization; today, most of its regular customers have moved farther west, in search of newer horizons— and country clubs.

And if there's a country club aura to the white frame building that houses Busch's Grove, it's because it serves as sort of an informal adjunct to many of them.

The outdoor gazebos are attractive and lovely for summer lunch and dinner, and the interior has the sort of formality and grace last seen in Pullman dining cars.

As far as dining is concerned, however, it's a mixed bag. Beef is the safest bet, with prime rib the safest of the safe, and salads for lunch. The kitchen doesn't seem equipped to experiment much, but then again, the current formula has worked for a long, long time.

165

CAFE MANHATTAN
511 South Hanley Rd.
(Clayton)
863-5695

>===

Cuisine: Modern American, pizza
Serves: Dinner, every day; lunch, Monday–Saturday
Prices: Inexpensive to moderate
Credit Cards: No credit cards
Dress: Informal
Reservations: Accepted
Handicap Access: Satisfactory
Separate No-Smoking Section: Yes

Bright and cheerful, with an old gasoline pump to keep watch over a soda fountain that doesn't make ice cream sodas, the Cafe Manhattan is a useful, handy place for lunch or a light dinner, with a menu that is universally American casual.

There are hamburgers, of course, and that old St. Louis favorite, Fitz' Kitchen Sauce, is available to help them. The sauce, once served at the late, lamented Fitz' Drive-In on Clayton Road, is tangy with Thousand Island dressing, pickle relish, and other good things.

Cafe Manhattan has good service and a large menu that includes my favorite style of pizza, with a thin crust and lots of available toppings—25 at last count—including great things like anchovies, bacon, sausage, fresh garlic, and mushrooms, and hair- curling things like artichokes, steamed spinach, zucchini, and broccoli.

Sandwiches are served on good whole-grain bread, and they're usually full enough to demand being eaten with knife and fork. The classic BLT is excellent, and the Reuben is prepared just right, with sourdough rye bread dotted with caraway seeds—the perfect host.

166

Alfalfa sprouts and tomato join the tuna fish, served on sourdough pumpernickel; and I was very happy with a Manhattan Club, where good braunschweiger replaces the turkey and adds a nifty touch. Italian meatballs, grilled chicken breast, and pastrami show the ethnic range of flavors.

An excellent Caesar salad tops a selection that also includes chef, seafood, and spinach salads.

Evening brings a few pasta dishes, including a vegetable lasagna, and the remainder of the menu also is available.

Beer and wine are served, and the dessert list includes cheesecake, carrot cake, and some ice cream delicacies, as well as a treat from the past—a good root beer float, with the root beer another Fitz legacy.

CAFE NAPOLI
21 South Bemiston Ave.
(Clayton)
863-5731

Cuisine: Italian
Serves: Dinner, Monday–Saturday; lunch, Monday–Friday
Prices: Inexpensive to moderate
Credit Cards: All major
Dress: Informal
Reservations: Accepted
Handicap Access: Difficult (few steps at entrance, narrow aisles)
Separate No-Smoking Section: Yes

Every St. Louis neighborhood has its neighborhood Italian restaurant, or two, or three. The Hill has them, cheek by jowl with more elegant spots, and so do all other areas. They have individual touches, but mostly they have similar menus featuring toasted ravioli or fried calimari appetizers, lots of pasta, and a good handful of veal and chicken dishes.

All have their fans, some for accessibility, others for a special dish or two, and all provide meals that are moderately priced, always satisfactory, and sometimes outstanding.

Cafe Napoli, small and paneled in light wood, does splendid things with pasta—led by a superior tortellini with peas in a rich cream sauce. Linguine with clam sauce is excellent, and so are pasta side dishes in a spicy tomato sauce. Beef and veal dishes are available under the usual variety of sauces.

Appetizers include a delightful shrimp de Jonghe, in a marinara-style sauce, and salads display a bright, well-balanced oil-and-vinegar dressing.

Desserts are led by a delightful, tart lemon ice that is a superb palate cleanser.

CAFE ZOE
12 North Meramec Ave. (Clayton)
725-5554

‹-›

Cuisine: Modern American
Serves: Dinner, Monday–Saturday; lunch, Monday–Friday
Prices: Lunch moderate, dinner expensive
Credit Cards: AE, MC, V
Dress: Informal, trendy
Reservations: Accepted and advised
Handicap Access: Satisfactory
Separate No-Smoking Section: Yes

It's a bright spot in Clayton now, but Cafe Zoe began under less auspicious circumstances in Lafayette Square, a popular area for rehabbers just south of downtown. It was an immediate success as the Empire Cafe, serving fresh, imaginative, delicious lunches.

Zoe Houk was a waitress there, and a good one. When the opportunity arose, she bought the restaurant, changed its name to match her own and made it an even greater success. Steve Robinson came on board, built a magnificent wine list, and married Zoe.

After a long search, they found a Clayton location and moved the operation—lock, stock, wine list, and chicken salad for lunch.

The new restaurant, opened in early 1991, has the same bright, airy look and the same comfortable feel as the old one. It remains extremely popular, and reservations are usually vital. The dinner menu has expanded, of course, while lunch brings the same dependable, delicious meals it always did. Service continues to be impeccable.

There's a California aura, not just in the cooking, but in the raw materials and the presentation too. Dishes tend to be on the light side, with sauces that avoid the heavy cream of haute cuisine.

There still is ample use of baby vegetables, which are pretty but, like babies, don't have much flavor. I prefer to talk to grown-ups and to eat grown-up vegetables.

Individual pizzas have proven a popular appetizer, but I much prefer the risotto—perfectly cooked and flavored with a splendid use of herbs. Soups are lovely, and a cream of onion is one of the best. Duck ravioli, served in a large, half-moon-shaped pasta, is a delight, and a delicate appetizer like carpaccio is treated with proper respect, with just a dollop of olive oil and a sprinkle of capers and shaved parmesan cheese atop lean, delicious beef that is allowed to show all its wonderful flavor without interference.

Speaking of olive oil, a flagon is on the table, ready for use with hearty, crusty homemade bread. Try it. It's a little sloppy, but far better than butter, and better for you, say some health experts. That's a group I agree with whenever their recommendations are the same as mine.

There are some beef entrees, and veal from time to time, but Cafe Zoe features fowl and fish. Fresh salmon, a mainstay from the Lafayette Square lunch menu, is poached or grilled, with a series of remarkable, light, tasty sauces. Fresh tuna is excellent too, but fish is often prepared on the rare side here, so if you want it well done, alert the server.

Roast duck is a longtime specialty, usually on the rare side too, but with exceptional fruit sauces and, on one recent visit, a roasted garlic sauce that was a delight. When garlic is roasted, it loses its bite and becomes more delicious than ever. The duck was accompanied by a garlic flan that had plenty of heat but was superb. Grilled chicken with roasted chile peppers was another outstanding example of a chef's imagination; the peppers still had some fire, and the chicken was perfectly cooked, flavored but not overheated by the chiles.

An array of vegetables comes alongside, including potatoes prepared according to the chef's mood and one or more of a group that could involve beets, carrots, leeks, spaghetti squash, zucchini, or whatever else the chef selects.

The wine list is long and lovely, with higher prices in the high-

170

rent neighborhood of Clayton, but still a wide range of selections at fair prices.

Desserts are excellent as well. A home-baked apple pie shows off classic simplicity. And a chocolate terrine—with white, medium, and dark chocolate—will satisfy, though I deny that there is such a thing as white chocolate; if it's white, it ain't chocolate. Crême brulée is not up to the standards set by other dishes.

CANDICCI'S
7910 Bonhomme Ave.
(Clayton)
725-3350

❖❖❖

Cuisine: Italian
Serves: Dinner, every day; lunch, Monday–Saturday
Prices: Moderate to expensive
Credit Cards: All major
Dress: Casual
Reservations: Accepted for parties of five or more
Handicap Access: Satisfactory
Separate No-Smoking Section: Yes

With more than two dozen pasta entrees available, this converted town house in the busy Clayton business district offers solid St. Louis–style Italian fare.

Pastas and salads are popular lunchtime choices, and well-prepared veal, chicken, and fish dishes, plus outstanding beef spidini, head the dinner selections.

Service is brisk, and while few dishes will stagger the imagination, everything that comes out of the kitchen is properly prepared and seasoned, and traditional recipes are treated with considerable respect. Desserts are homemade.

CARDWELL'S
8100 Maryland Ave. (Clayton)
726-5055

<hr>

Cuisine: American Modern
Serves: Lunch and dinner, every day
Prices: Expensive to very expensive
Credit Cards: AE, MC, V
Dress: Informal
Reservations: Accepted, necessary on weekends
Handicap Access: Satisfactory
Separate No-Smoking Section: Yes

A large number of restaurants open strong, like horses that come flying out of the starting gate. Unfortunately, many fade at the clubhouse turn and disappear by the time they reach the back stretch.

Cardwell's is a great exception. It opened in 1987 with such a burst of speed that I referred to it as "Rookie of the Year" in the first edition of this book. No longer a rookie, Cardwell's has maintained high standards and continues to be a leader among St. Louis restaurants.

It has also led the way in helping to upgrade the restaurants of Clayton, catering to the movers and shakers of St. Louis County. The ground-floor location in a high-rise office building opens onto patio space for summer lunches, and the dining room attracts a wide-ranging clientele. The bar can get noisy at peak hours, and so can the front dining areas, but the darker, more elegant room to the rear is quieter.

The style is Modern American but avoids fussiness. Chef Bill Cardwell has a splendid imagination to accompany fine technique, along with a real talent for matching food and wine. His preparation of wild game and other unusual items is superior, and many dishes are not seen anywhere else in the area.

The menu changes from season to season, always featuring the freshest produce and seafood, brilliant sauces, and exemplary entrees and desserts, plus a large, intelligently selected wine list with some excellent values.

The appetizer list involves a variety of homemade pâtés and sausages, smoked wild turkey, prosciutto made from wild boar, and a dish as simple as black-eyed peas in a lovely vinaigrette dressing. A spectacular cream soup is based on five onions—leeks, red onions, white onions, scallions, and tiny pearl onions—and is a glorious taste experience. Rabbit terrine is rich and tasty, and duck sausage is wonderful, with the duck flavor peering through here and there, under a delectable garnish of plum chutney.

There are moments—not often, thankfully—when the kitchen gets carried away, as in an endive salad that included pink grapefruit, goat cheese, pomegranate seeds, and a chive dressing, far too many disparate flavors for a single dish.

Basic steaks and chops are included among the entrees, but the list is heavy on fish and fowl, and preparation can range from simple to complex. A simple sautéd lemon sole in fresh tomatoes and fennel was just right, while sweetbreads in a Chardonnay sauce, with leeks and shiitake mushrooms, went to the other extreme and arrived with melt-in-the-mouth texture and an extraordinary blend of flavors.

Calf's liver, with polenta as a side dish, was cooked to perfect tenderness and peak flavor. Duck breast, rubbed with pepper, cooked medium rare, and sliced thin, displayed a lovely tang of pepper that complemented the dark taste of the duck in elegant style.

The wine list can match any entree, and the desserts are outstanding, led by a dark chocolate soufflé with bourbon and pecans that was as light, fluffy, and flavorful as any I've ever eaten. The pastries are not to be ignored, but the soufflé is a crowning glory.

CARL'S DRIVE-IN
9033 Manchester Rd.
(Rock Hill)
961-3663

❖❖❖

Cuisine: Hamburgers and trimmings
Serves: Lunch and dinner, Monday–Saturday
Prices: Inexpensive
Credit Cards: No credit cards
Dress: Casual
Reservations: Not applicable
Handicap Access: Difficult
Separate No-Smoking Section: No

"Hamburgers, hot dogs, root beer, and memories served here," is what the sign in front of Carl's Drive-In should say. The 16-seat (8 on each side) spot in Rock Hill dates at least to 1929, when now-busy Manchester Road was gravel.

It's a real throwback, a fond reminiscence of days when every small community in the United States had at least two drive-in diners—one at each end of town. It's a nifty place for a quick, casual lunch or to take the children and grandchildren and regale them with tales of old times.

Owner Frank Cunetto is proud of his home-brewed root beer—up to 60 gallons a day in the summer, drawn from an antique barrel that dominates the minuscule place, and served in frosted mugs. Customers appreciate his attention to detail; hamburgers go onto the grill, and potatoes into the fryer, only after they're ordered, so everything is fresh and hot, and the small burgers remain juicy.

Hot dogs (including a hot dog Reuben with sauerkraut on whole-wheat bread) are good, and there are also chicken breasts, pork steaks, fish sandwiches, and chili. A root beer float makes a splendid dessert, and Cunetto usually has Ron Ryan's best-in-town sorbet too.

CASA GALLARDO GRILL
Saint Louis Galleria
Brentwood Boulevard at Clayton Road
(Richmond Heights)
727-2223

❖❖

Cuisine: Mexican–Southwestern American
Serves: Lunch and dinner, every day
Prices: Moderate to expensive
Credit Cards: All major
Dress: Informal
Reservations: Accepted
Handicap Access: Satisfactory
Separate No-Smoking Section: Yes

The expanded Galleria became the city's fanciest shopping center when it opened in the summer of 1991. For those who eat, rather than those who shop, the Casa Gallardo Grill is one of its most welcome tenants.

The food is Mexican–Southwestern American, with good touches of spicing that reflect the marriage between the two cultures, and service is plentiful and professional. It's a large, somewhat noisy room, with no view except that of the center's parking lot, but it's bright and cheerful. A large, busy bar fills about a fourth of the squarish room, and the remainder forms an 'L' shape around it.

Maybe it's a little bit of a gimmick, but the Grill's technique of making guacamole tableside is a great idea, providing fresh guacamole spiced to the diner's desire. The serving person arrives with fresh, ripe avocados and peels and mashes them with a fork, offering a variety of spices and adding them as requested. The result is a dish of superior texture and flavor, the perfect companion to a margarita.

176

Two excellent salsas are on every table, a red with a good pop, and a darker, interesting green with backtastes of cilantro and, perhaps, some chocolate. Standard chips are good; blue ones look like slate and are about as tender. Soft tortillas are fresh and outstanding.

Ceviche, or marinated raw fish in a spicy, lemony sauce, is also splendid; so are crab cakes in a jalapeño-butter sauce that is piquant but not hot. Blue corn taco shells filled with duck don't show enough flavor.

Delicious black beans accompany all entrees, which are led by various combinations of enchiladas, hard and soft tacos, and burritos. Chicken enchiladas, with a spicy cream sauce, were the most exciting.

More interesting, and tastier, are items like carnitas, or marinated pork baked in banana leaves, which comes out with a series of rich tastes, like great barbecue, only different. Fajitas are good, with grilled beef, chicken, and shrimp all showing excellent flavor, and the various sauces are good complements that don't overpower. Chile relleño has lots of cheese but not much personality. Various vegetables come alongside, including jicama, a tasty root that looks like a turnip but is far more flavorful.

Desserts include a high-grade carrot cake, and one of the most interesting presentations I've ever seen—something that looked exactly like an ear of white corn, kernels and all. It's a dark chocolate mousse inside a white chocolate shell, and while the dark is better than the white, the dish is very good, and almost too pretty to eat.

CHARCOAL HOUSE
9855 Manchester Blvd.
(Rock Hill)
968-4842

❖───❖

Cuisine: Steaks
Serves: Dinner, Monday–Saturday; lunch, Monday–Friday
Prices: Moderate to expensive
Credit Cards: AE, MC, V
Dress: Informal
Reservations: Accepted on weekdays only
Handicap Access: Satisfactory
Separate No-Smoking Section: No

Food fads come and go. Food zealots come and go. The Charcoal House, however, continues as a popular, midpriced restaurant where steak is always in fashion. There is more fish on the menu than there once was, but the small frame building remains a beacon for those in search of beef.

There is good beef to be found here, with chateaubriand, T-bone, sirloin, and filet mignon leading the way. All are delicious, arriving at table cooked just the way they're ordered, tender and flavorful.

The appetizer list is small, but soups are good and salads better. The Charcoal House prepares a superior Caesar salad and an exemplary spinach salad, both with crisp, fresh greens and a pleasing dressing. The spinach is bolstered with real bacon, hard-boiled egg, and mushroom slices, and the dressing is light. The standard house salad is well above average.

Fish is well prepared, too. The grilled grouper is delicious—slightly charred outside, soft and delicious inside.

My only problem at the Charcoal House is that the good steaks deserve better potatoes. Baked ones arrive in foil, which immediately chills my soul, and hashed browns have been dry and tough on occasion. The wine list is small, offering a few pleasant reds to go with the steaks. A few more would be nice. Desserts are simple and satisfactory.

CHEZ LOUIS
26 North Meramec Ave.
(Clayton)
863-8400

❖❖

Cuisine: French
Serves: Dinner, Monday–Saturday; lunch, Monday–Friday
Prices: Expensive to very expensive
Credit Cards: All major
Dress: Jackets preferred
Reservations: Accepted, necessary on weekends
Handicap Access: Satisfactory
Separate No-Smoking Section: Yes

Chez Louis has been at a crossroads recently, but seems to be turning in the proper direction, which would be backward—backward, that is, to its glory days of the first edition of this book.

At that time, it had been one of the city's finest French restaurants and had improved when the Seven Gables Hotel was built around and over it, making Chez Louis a fine hotel's fine dining room. Upon the arrival of the hotel, the restaurant decor shifted a little, from gallery posters to slightly more formal hangings.

The death of Morton Meyer, who had been the restaurant's guiding light, and a too-rapid turnover of chefs, left Chez Louis rather rudderless. Michael Holmes has taken over as executive chef, and things seem to be moving in the right direction. A recent visit was outstanding, and Holmes is showing flair, imagination, and a winning touch. I think the loyal audience is still there, but many others—like me—are hoping that this is a good omen for the future.

COUSIN HUGO'S
3233 Laclede Station Rd.
(Maplewood)
645-8484

❖═══❖

Cuisine: Bar fare
Serves: Lunch and dinner, Monday–Saturday (same menu)
Prices: Inexpensive
Credit Cards: MC, V
Dress: Casual
Reservations: Not applicable
Handicap Access: Satisfactory
Separate No-Smoking Section: No

Despite its location on a busy city street, Cousin Hugo's one-story, white frame building, with satellite dish alongside, gives it the look and feel of a classic roadhouse. It's basically a bar with food service, though it achieved some fame when local author Glenn Savan used it as an important meeting place—complete with foreplay—in his novel *White Palace.*

When moviemakers wanted to use it for the film version, the ownership refused permission, preferring to keep it open for the regular clientele, so a South City bar was used instead.

Like many St. Louis bars, Cousin Hugo's offers hamburgers and sandwiches. The flat-grill hamburgers, with onions cooked alongside if you like, are very tasty. The flat grill results in a burger that is slightly greasier than those cooked on an open grill, but there are times when the human system—like the automotive one—needs greasing.

There are some other sandwiches, soups, and chili, and barbecued ribs, pork steaks, and chicken on weekends.

CYRANO'S
1059 South Big Bend Blvd.
(Richmond Heights)
645-3522

Cuisine: American
Serves: Dinner, every day; lunch, Monday–Friday
Prices: Inexpensive to moderate
Credit Cards: MC, V
Dress: Casual
Reservations: Accepted
Handicap Access: Satisfactory
Separate No-Smoking Section: No

A St. Louis dessert-and-coffee tradition for many years, Cyrano's has been host to thousands of post-movie and post-prom dates in its time. Giant ice cream concoctions are its stock in trade.

There's also a lunch and dinner service, including some dishes from recipes left behind when Richard Perry moved to Cincinnati. Whether the cooks at Cyrano's are as capable as the chefs at Perry's is a big question, however. The regular menu usually results in inconsistent meals, and service is a weak point.

THE DINING ROOM AND THE GRILL
Ritz-Carlton Hotel
1 Ritz-Carlton Drive
(Clayton)
863-6300

Cuisine: French-American
Serves: Breakfast, lunch, and dinner, every day
Prices: Expensive to very expensive
Credit Cards: All major
Dress: Jackets preferred for men
Reservations: Accepted
Handicap Access: Satisfactory
Separate No-Smoking Section: Yes

The Ritz-Carlton Hotel towers over Clayton like a monument to privilege—its own exit from the Forsyth Bypass, its own traffic light at the Hanley Road entrance, gleaming brass everywhere.

Without question, it's an elegant place. Its two restaurants, The Grill and The Dining Room are lovely, the former in dark paneling, the latter light and bright, with plenty of sun and a soothing airiness. As a personal aside, I can't abide the capitalization of a definite article in a pretentious effort to convert the ordinary into the extra-ordinary.

The two restaurants share their top chefs and some of the same dishes are on both menus. The wine lists and the dessert carts are identical.

Like all restaurants, those at the Ritz set their standards with their prices, and both are very high. I've had problems with carelessness in some dishes, though others have been superlative. A matchless porterhouse steak and rivaling crab cakes are served at the Grill. And a wonderful corn chowder with bits of roast duck, plus a splendid chicken breast stuffed with wild mushrooms, spinach, garlic, and thyme can be found at the Dining Room.

Desserts are impeccable, with both presentation and flavor of the highest caliber.

Some personnel changes have undoubtedly hampered the kitchen at the Ritz-Carlton, but its restaurants are as elegant as any in the area; and when they're right, they're very, very right. At their prices, however, it's sometimes difficult to gamble.

EUROPEAN CAFFE'
8064 Clayton Rd.
(Richmond Heights)
727-2383

❖━❖

Cuisine: Italian
Serves: Lunch and dinner, Monday–Saturday
Prices: Moderate to expensive
Credit Cards: All major
Dress: Informal
Reservations: Accepted
Handicap Access: Satisfactory
Separate No-Smoking Section: Yes

Despite recession, winter, and a variety of other ill omens, St. Louis restaurateurs spent 1991 challenging Rodgers and Hammerstein's Nellie Forbush for "cockeyed optimist" honors. Rita Weaver, who has another European Caffe' in University City, opened this larger and more elegant spot late in the year, with an Italian menu and a lovely touch with herbs and spices.

There are French overtones to some of the dishes, and a pleasing lightness to almost everything.

Appetizers include the Italian rice ball, arancini, rolled with herbs, bread crumbs, and pieces of salami, then fried. They're very tasty, though a little heavy for an appetizer. Seafood bisque is lovely; tender flash-fried squid offers an exemplary batter; and ceviche, or marinated fish, shrimp, or scallops, is excellent, with a pleasing, tangy, citrus-tinted marinade.

Salads and vegetables accompany the entrees. Salads of fresh, tasty greens are topped by superior homemade dressings: the house specialty, a creamy artichoke-mushroom, is deliciously light, and a tomato-basil is tangy and impressive.

Entrees were in the same class. Chicken, with a vinegar

185

marinade in the Venetian style, was tender and juicy inside a skin that showed the vinegar in perfect balance. Grilled shrimp, served on a bed of sautéd onions with feta cheese chunks here and there, brought a set of different taste sensations. Veal in a pizzaiola sauce, heavy with oregano, capers, and garlic, was outstanding.

The wine list is modest but offers some nice accompaniments; service is good, though it tended to be slightly cloying in the restaurant's early days—a problem that is easily solved.

The dessert tray offers an attractive selection, with a blackberry chocolate mousse cake the most satisfactory. Key lime cheesecake can't hold a candle to Key lime pie, but it's a nice effort. It's early, but the European Caffe' seems to be ready to claim a high niche in the local restaurant market.

FIO'S LA FOURCHETTE
1153 St. Louis Galleria
Brentwood Boulevard at Clayton Road
(Richmond Heights)
863-6866

❖❖❖

Cuisine: French
Serves: Dinner, Tuesday–Saturday
Prices: Expensive to very expensive
Credit Cards: AE, MC, V
Dress: Jackets preferred
Reservations: Accepted and advised
Handicap Access: Satisfactory
Separate No-Smoking Section: No

A gourmet restaurant in a shopping mall may sound like an oxymoron, but Fio's La Fourchette ("Fio's Fork" in French) has almost completely overcome the problem with its own parking area and a location that—with a little use of the imagination—can make one forget.

A long list of wondrous sensations comes from the kitchen of Swiss-born Fio Antognini and his wife, Lisa, in an elegant, pink-tinted room that offers relaxed, delightful dining at a level to match the city's highest.

The cuisine blends haute and nouvelle with a superior imagination, a loving touch, and perfect preparation and presentation. Fio's has three menus too: a standard à la carte, a list light in calories and fats (including a molasses soufflé with only 107 calories), and a fixed-price tasting menu that includes a little bit of almost everything. And, if none of those possibilities satisfy, you can mix and match from anything on any menu.

In addition, Fio's offers second portions—something almost unheard-of in a lovely and expensive French restaurant. Think about loving every bite of an appetizer, say, of perfectly matched, perfectly chilled mussels in a light, tangy, delectable ginger-and-cream sauce, and then having the waiter stroll by and offer a few more.

The Antogninis explained to me once that they'd rather do it this way than serve too much, make some diners uncomfortable and have food left over, and it's a grand gesture.

I've never had a dish I didn't like at Fio's, though some have been more thrilling than others, and I've also never seen a dish where the presentation fell short of display quality.

Tortellini filled with escargot is a glorious appetizer that is a dish for the Antogninis' heritage—a taste combination symbolizing the position of Switzerland right between France and Italy. Homemade pâtés and sausages are tangy and beautifully textured and everything is accompanied by a sauce that is the ideal complement—or compliment—if you prefer.

Soups are in the same style; I'm particularly fond of a clam bisque that blends whole clams in a rich, smooth broth and adds bits of julienned vegetables for texture as well as flavor.

Beef Wellington is as well prepared here as I've ever tasted it; juicy beef, a layer of soft, rich pâté, and a crisp pastry are all just right, and blend in lovely style. Lamb and veal receive creative treatment, and Fio's prepares a red snapper stuffed with tiny shrimp and smoked oysters that is a taste sensation. Game in season is always spectacular.

The wine list is deep with French and California offerings, and there are some Swiss wines too—in honor of the owners' heritage. The Swiss wines are adequate, and well made, but they don't have the body of their French or American counterparts.

Desserts are the perfect ending to the meal, and while I'm a traditional Grand Marnier soufflé fancier—and Fio's prepares a marvelous one—I have succumbed to the lure of an Irish coffee soufflé, with a wonderful hit of Irish whiskey and a huge dollop of whipped cream.

Fio's La Fourchette is truly an elegant restaurant, in every sense of the word.

GIRARROSTO
101 South Hanley Rd.
(Clayton)
726-4900

❖❖❖

Cuisine: Italian bistro
Serves: Dinner, every day; lunch, Monday–Friday
Prices: Moderate to expensive
Credit Cards: All major
Dress: Informal
Reservations: Accepted
Handicap Access: Satisfactory
Separate No-Smoking Section: Yes

We already have just about all the Italian restaurants we can handle in St. Louis—and some are great ones, too—so it takes a certain amount of courage to open another, but if it's a solid value, with perhaps a twist or two, there's a good chance for success.

So it is with Girarrosto, a mostly Italian bistro, with some American touches, that seems to have settled down in the Clayton space once occupied, with disastrous results, by the Dierdorf & Hart group.

The room still doesn't work very well; a lovely grill stands between the bar area and the dining room, but supplies must be taken to it, and trash removed from it, by staff members carrying things through the dining room. However, the decor has been made more friendly, and the addition of awnings to bring color to the room is a nice touch.

Tables are covered with butcher paper and crayons are available—a concept that went out of date about the time pocket calculators arrived. While I was there one night, the waiter wrote the specials on it—a satisfactory idea except that his spelling was atrocious. Believe it or not, in an Italian restaurant, the waiter misspelled *spaghetti*.

My editor's black heart wanted to correct it on the spot (or the table), but I knew he would see it, and it would embarrass him. My alternate thought was to tear it off, give it to him and demand he bring it back tomorrow with his mother's signature, but that would have been worse. It also reminded me of the time I saw a young Cardinal football player misspell his own name on his very first autograph request, but that's still another story.

The menu is designed for mixing and matching, with appetizers, crostini, several pastas of the day, sandwiches, and grilled entrees. Olive oil arrives with bread, a combination that makes butter seem third-rate, and the crostini is excellent, involving crisp toast with a variety of toppings, including roasted eggplant and peppers, tapenade (olives and sun-dried tomatoes), caponata (eggplant and tomatoes), and excellent chopped chicken liver.

Stuffed squid is a tasty appetizer, with carpaccio less so, and polenta with mushrooms and roasted garlic is a delight.

Entrees include delicious, moist, tender grilled chicken, and splendid, herb-tasty grilled lamb. Sausage, heavy with fennel, made a superior complement to polenta.

The wine list has some fine and moderately priced Italian varieties, and a good selection of California labels.

Desserts include a superior tiramisu, with a proper balance of liqueur and excellent cake, and a winning, crisp, cold, tart lemon ice. Service is good—since the ability to spell has little to do with the basics of serving—and the restaurant has a robust charm.

HACIENDA
9748 Manchester
(Rock Hill)
962-7100

❖-❖

Cuisine: Mexican
Serves: Dinner, every day; lunch, Monday–Saturday
Prices: Inexpensive to moderate
Credit Cards: All major
Dress: Casual
Reservations: Accepted
Handicap Access: Satisfactory
Separate No-Smoking Section: Yes

Passable Mexican food—and lots of it—keeps this ultraordinary restaurant popular, and usually crowded, but the kitchen of this large, sprawling, casual dining spot lacks creativity and imagination.

The usual Tex-Mex dishes—tacos, enchiladas, and burritos—are on the menu and are adequate, but nothing special.

HSU'S CHINESE RESTAURANT
9626 Olive Blvd.
(Olivette)
569-0925

✦✦✦

Cuisine: Chinese
Serves: Lunch and dinner, every day
Prices: Moderate to expensive
Credit Cards: All major
Dress: Informal
Reservations: Accepted
Handicap Access: Satisfactory
Separate No-Smoking Section: Yes

Tom Hsu, a great chef who took advantage of many people—including me—cooked at or operated a half-dozen or so restaurants during his first St. Louis tenure, convincing many that each was going to be his career stop before using his plaudits and clippings to sell the place and move on.

He left his name on just one—a venerable location in Olivette that has continued to provide better-than-average meals from a menu of almost infinite variety. In addition, there's an entire Cantonese menu, heavy with seafood, that is available on request.

The standard menu is large, but with some nice touches like real lobster Cantonese style, frog legs, duck with ginger, and oysters with black bean sauce.

It even offers "chicken steak," though it's pan-fried chicken, probably in the shape of steak (whatever shape that is) and served in the chef's special sauce.

Egg rolls, scallion pancakes, dumplings (pot-stickers), and shrimp toast are outstanding appetizers. Clams in black bean sauce and some noodle dishes make elegant entrees from the Cantonese menu.

HUNAN WOK

2428 South Brentwood Blvd.
(Brentwood)

962-0898

Cuisine: Chinese
Serves: Lunch and dinner, every day
Prices: Moderate to expensive
Credit Cards: AE, MC, V
Dress: Casual
Reservations: Accepted
Handicap Access: Satisfactory
Separate No-Smoking Section: Yes

Szechuan and Hunan cooking has become a major part of St. Louis cuisine since the mid-1970s, but owners and chefs entered a time warp a half-dozen years ago, and nothing has changed since. The result is a large number of Chinese restaurants like the Hunan Wok—similar menus, similar preparation, and nothing special.

Most of the establishments do a few things very well; the problem is that the successful dishes vary, depending on who's in charge in the kitchen, and this city's Asiatic chefs have jumped from place to place in a fashion that sheds nothing but disgrace either on them or their employers. It's difficult to determine exactly where the blame belongs.

So the Hunan Wok is no different from many other locations. It provides satisfactory fare, but without much imagination and with a style similar to its counterparts.

Pot-stickers, or dumplings, have been excellent, and so are cold noodles and shrimp toast. Shrimp and pork entrees are satisfactory, though tough meat has caused a problem with many of the beef entrees.

Dinners are adequate and, when the urge for this cuisine strikes, the Hunan Wok does a satisfactory job.

JOE & CHARLIE'S
8040 Clayton Rd.
(Richmond Heights)
721-9597

Cuisine: American bar fare
Serves: Lunch and dinner, every day
Prices: Inexpensive
Credit Cards: None
Dress: Casual
Reservations: Not applicable
Handicap Access: Entry satisfactory, rest rooms difficult (stairs)
Separate No-Smoking Section: No

When Joe & Charlie's was young, some 35 years ago, it was a raucous attraction of Gaslight Square, with ragtime music, a long bar, and sawdust on the floor. As it matured, it moved west, but its Brentwood Boulevard location was a hangout for athletes and St. Patrick's Day revelers. Now, as it nears middle age, it is a sometimes quiet spot on Clayton Road, very busy with bu businessmen for lunch and home to a good sampling of bowlers, softball players, waiters, lawyers, and other degenerates later at night.

The bar is not as long, but it's well stocked and friendly.

The small kitchen provides superior bar food. Sandwiches are well stuffed—the Reuben is hot and tangy, the Poor Boy is filling, and high-grade braunschweiger on good rye, with a slice of onion, is memorable. Salads are good too. Most items are available as late as midnight.

The chili is better than most bar chilies; a little hot sauce is all it needs. In a more experimental era, when Dick Bland was behind the bar, it often was improved (he said) with thingsngs like mushrooms and black olives, but that was a long time ago, and we all were more understanding.

KEN BARRY'S RESTAURANT & LOUNGE
8428 Olive Blvd.
(University City)
993-6619

✧✧✧

Cuisine: American
Serves: Dinner, Monday–Saturday; lunch, Monday–Friday
Prices: Inexpensive to moderate
Credit Cards: MC, Visa
Dress: Informal
Reservations: Only for parties of six or more
Handicap Access: Difficult (narrow aisles)
Separate No-Smoking Section: No

Time was, when legendary trenchermen ruled the earth, that turtle soup was an integral part of almost every St. Louis restaurant menu, served at both lunch and dinner, always with a dollop of sherry on top or alongside.

Times change, however, and turtle soup is now found only on rare occasions. At Ken Barry's, turtle soup is a regular—rich and delicious, with sherry alongside.

Barry, once a popular singer, has been running a successful restaurant and bar for many years, and he has a large and loyal clientele. The reason is simple—good food, simply prepared, at prices that make it a good value.

It's a small place, reminiscent of places that used to exist everywhere but were invaded, and eventually smothered, by ferns, fancy drinks, and trendy food.

Barry does excellent steaks, chops, and fish items, and always has beef brisket available, which sets him apart. The brisket is cooked a long time, making it tender and flaky, and it's served as a

195

sandwich on a fresh French roll, or on a plate with natural gravy or tangy barbecue sauce alongside.

Homemade pies head the dessert list.

KING DOH
10045 Manchester Blvd.
(Warson Woods)
821-6988

❖•❖

Cuisine: Chinese
Serves: Dinner, Tuesday–Sunday; lunch, Tuesday–Friday
Prices: Moderate
Credit Cards: AE, MC, V
Reservations: Accepted
Handicap Access: Satisfactory
Separate No-Smoking Section: No

One of the area's more enjoyable Chinese restaurants, this small storefront establishment has a loyal clientele that is willing to trade imaginative, different cooking for consistency and freshness—not always a bad swap. Nothing is highly dramatic, but everything tastes good.

The menu is much like so many Chinese establishments, but everything on it is prepared the way it should be and arrives quickly from the kitchen. In addition, there's a satisfactory Cantonese-style selection.

The traditional Cantonese dish of shrimp in lobster sauce is rich and delightfully garlicky. The side dish of snow peas and black mushrooms is outstanding, heaped with tasty mushrooms and crisp snow peas. It is a vegetarian's delight.

Among the spicier items, Mongolian beef shows better beef than many similar establishments. It is sliced thick, is tender, and has considerable flavor of its own. Spicing is proper, as it is in Kung Pao chicken, where the red pepper is present but not overpowering.

Egg roll and shrimp toast lead the largely traditional (in the American sense) appetizer list.

KOH-I-NOOR
608 Eastgate Ave.
(University City)
721-3796

Cuisine: Pakistani
Serves: Dinner, Tuesday–Saturday; lunch, Tuesday–Friday
Prices: Inexpensive to moderate
Credit Cards: All major
Dress: Informal
Reservations: Accepted
Handicap Access: Passable
Separate No-Smoking Section: Yes

Koh-I-Noor brought Pakistani cuisine to St. Louis 15 years ago, first to a storefront in Overland, later to a pair of University City Loop locations. It's sometimes difficult to believe that the time has passed so quickly.

The present location, just off busy Delmar Boulevard, is smaller than its former one, but I think it's the most attractive of all, with soft gray walls and some brass hangings bringing a warm, comfortable feeling.

Meals from the subcontinent of India range from mild to ultra-spicy, and Koh-I-Noor's seems mostly on the mild side, though I'm sure they can be more throat-burning by request. By the way, most dishes come with a side of cucumbers in yogurt, and they're the most cooling thing I know if you make a mistake.

Most meals start with papadamus, a paper-thin fried bread dotted with lentils and spicy cardamom seeds, and I find it more insidious than Cracker Jacks. Naan, much like pita, also is served.

Appetizers include various samosas, or turnovers—fresh and flaky fried pastry dough filled with combinations like peas and potatoes, or meat and potatoes. Fried eggplant is topped with a delicious piquant yogurt sauce. Rice cakes with yogurt and tomatoes are also tasty.

A Koh-I-Noor favorite of mine is nargisi kofta, which is similar to the Scotch egg served in English pubs. It's a hard-boiled egg rolled in spicy ground beef, and I think it's splendid.

Entrees involve some pleasingly sharp curries, with lamb, chicken, or shrimp, and the curry involves homemade blending of various spices (cumin, pepper, cardamom, and others) that are ground together to make what we see as "curry powder" on the supermarket shelf.

There are also some combination dishes that have, say, one piece of roast chicken with pilau rice, and a second piece in curry sauce. The curry is nice on both the chicken and the vegetables. Stuffed eggplant is much like the comparable dish of most cultures, but Koh-I-Noor's is slightly spicier.

Two types of chutney—sweet-and-sour or hot—come alongside, and both live up to their descriptions.

A variety of sweet cakes are the dessert choices. Gulabjamom, spiced with cardamom, wrapped in silver paper, and served with a sweet sauce, is a tasty one.

MAI LEE
8440 Delmar Blvd.
(University City)
993-3754

❖❖❖

Cuisine: Vietnamese/Chinese
Serves: Lunch and dinner, Tuesday–Sunday
Prices: Inexpensive to moderate
Credit Cards: All major
Dress: Casual
Reservations: Accepted
Handicap Access: Satisfactory
Separate No-Smoking Section: Yes

Mai Lee was one of the first restaurants to bring Vietnamese cooking to St. Louis. From an unprepossessing location, it serves delicious, inexpensive dishes with some rich, spicy flavors that tingle the tongue.

There's a Chinese menu too, but I've never tried it, preferring the lightly spiced Vietnamese dishes that show more influence of lemongrass and coriander (also known as cilantro) than anything else. Garlic is also prevalent, and there is major use of peanuts, which usually indicates the presence of red pepper as well.

There are hot and cold rolled appetizers—a hot egg roll with a lot of tangy pork, and a cold one, wrapped in rice paper and stuffed with shrimp, pork, and vegetables, including cucumbers and green onions.

Soups are superior and can almost double as entrees. Rice noodles with roast pork and shrimp arrive in a soup with noodles and bean sprouts, and vermicelli with barbecued pork offers a thicker noodle and smoky, delicious meat.

Curried chicken and spicy (very spicy) squid were excellent, but some beef and chicken dishes were hampered by tough meat.

Frog chunks with vegetables and curry sauce were delicious, if a far cry from the frog legs I'm familiar with.

Fruit drinks and Vietnamese iced coffee are delightful, especially in the summer.

THE MANDARIN HOUSE
65 Town and Country Mall
Page Blvd. and Woodson Rd.
(Overland)
427-8070

❖❖❖

Cuisine: Chinese
Serves: Lunch and dinner, every day
Prices: Inexpensive to moderate
Credit Cards: All major
Dress: Casual
Reservations: Accepted
Handicap Access: Satisfactory
Separate No-Smoking Section: Yes

The menu is one of the largest in the area, and there's a most impressive needlepoint picture of the Great Wall of China, but not much else about the Mandarin House sets it apart from the city's other Chinese restaurants.

The cooking is pleasant, if not imaginative. Appetizers like moo shu pork and pot-stickers are fresh and tasty, but the entrees have only proven adequate or less.

Too many dishes advertised as spicy-hot are not prepared that way; they're all basically mild with some red peppers tossed in at the last minute. If you bite into one, it's very hot, but food should include seasoning from the beginning of the process.

At the same time, Mandarin special noodles are tasty, and kung pao chicken, with peanuts and vegetables, has been satisfactory.

No one goes away hungry, either. Portions are huge, and everything is served piping hot. Good meals, just not exciting ones.

202

MAX'S BAR & GRILL
112 South Bemiston Ave.
(Clayton)
721-3443

❖-❖

Cuisine: American
Serves: Lunch and dinner daily, brunch on Sunday
Prices: Moderate
Credit Cards: All major
Dress: Casual
Reservations: Accepted
Handicap Access: Passable (few steps to bar)
Separate No-Smoking Section: Yes

A newcomer to the Hanon group of restaurants and part of Clayton's Radisson Hotel, where Hanon also operates the main dining room, this handsome bar and grill opened late in 1991 to seek a share of the Clayton lunch business.

The fare is very American, with steaks and chops, a couple of pasta dishes, pizza, a Cajun offering, and some Mexican appetizers—the new American menu. That's not a knock, but just an acknowledgment of how American restaurateurs have adapted to ethnic cuisine by adopting many different dishes.

Preparation is proper, and service is bright and professional.

Specialty breads have become popular in the last year or two, and Max's uses a two-tone rye for a superior Reuben, made with pastrami instead of the traditional corned beef, but with excellent balance among meat, cheese, kraut, sauce, and bread. It's rare when one can taste all five ingredients in a Reuben, but it happens here.

Hamburgers are large and freshly made, with good french fries, and salads show crisp, tasty greens and pleasing dressings. Chili is passable, but without a proper tang, and scallop chowder begins with a clam chowder base, which hurts its taste.

NOBU'S JAPANESE RESTAURANT
8643 Olive Blvd.
(University City)
997-2303

❖❖❖

Cuisine: Japanese
Serves: Dinner, daily; lunch, Monday–Friday; closed Wednesday
Prices: Moderate (expensive only if you stuff yourself with sushi)
Credit Cards: All major
Dress: Casual
Reservations: Only for parties of five or more
Handicap Access: Satisfactory
Separate No-Smoking Section: No smoking in restaurant

One of the problems with restaurant design is that people who run the restaurant don't eat there like regular customers, nor are they built like regular customers. Nobu Kidera is a brilliant sushi chef, but he's a short man who could fit easily into the minuscule booths or at the tiny sushi bar area of his first St. Louis restaurant.

For most other people, it was a real chore.

Kidera has a new restaurant now, in much larger, more comfortable quarters, with a larger menu and meals that are better than ever. Nobu's Japanese Restaurant is one of the best of its type in the area.

The chef continues to work wonders; his flashing knife and quick hands arrange fish onto sushi or sashimi platters that look like displays ready to be photographed, and everything is fresh and delicious.

The larger kitchen provides for an expanded choice of entrees, featuring more seafood and traditional Japanese dishes to go with popular American meals of sukiyaki or tempura. The former brings strips of tender beef, bean curd, spices, vegetables, noodles, and other goodies steaming together in a rich, delicious broth.

Tempura, or shrimp and vegetables in a melt-in-the-mouth batter, quickly fried, is delicious, the flavors of the vegetables shining through.

An occasional language barrier with the serving personnel makes it difficult to find out exactly what is what. Mackerel in a miso sauce, based on soybean paste, was slightly salty but very flavorful. Grilled squid or broiled beef with ginger sauce is splendid, and so are fried oysters. Grilled salmon and some of the dishes that end up in soup bowls, much like a seafood stew, are tasty.

Japanese bouillabaisse, involving scallops, shrimp, soft fish, black mushrooms, celery cabbage, yam noodles, and onions offers a variety of textures and flavors.

LA PATISSERIE
6269 Delmar Blvd.
(University City)
725-4902

❖❖❖

Cuisine: American, with French overtones
Serves: Breakfast and lunch, every day
Prices: Inexpensive to moderate
Credit Cards: None
Dress: Casual
Reservations: Not applicable
Handicap Access: Satisfactory
Separate No-Smoking Section: No

La Patisserie began as a pastry shop and coffeehouse but has grown into a stylish, interesting breakfast and lunch stop, with an imaginative menu that makes healthy raw material taste good. It's a small storefront, with considerable charm, and a hint of 1950s San Francisco in its operation.

Soups are excellent, thin-crust vegetarian pizza is a winner, barbecued tofu is not. Chicken salad and smoked turkey are delightful, usually in delicious combinations on superior bread. Vegetable stir-fry is nicely spiced. And quiche is exemplary, regardless of the filling; it arrives piping hot, rich, and creamy, and tastes the way a quiche should taste, and not like the cardboard box too many resemble.

The breakfast menu shows such interesting items as French toast with orange-apricot sauce, English crumpets, and Irish oatmeal. Croissants are fresh and warm, and pastries are elegant.

THE RED SEA
6511 Delmar Blvd.
(University City)
863-0099

❖❖

Cuisine: Ethiopian
Serves: Dinner, every night; lunch, Wednesday–Saturday
Prices: Inexpensive to moderate
Credit Cards: None
Dress: Casual
Reservations: Accepted (parties of three or more on weekends)
Handicap Access: Satisfactory
Separate No-Smoking Section: Yes

The area's first—and only—Ethiopian restaurant, which fits right into the international aura of the establishments in the University City Loop, provides inexpensive meals and the chance to sample a whole new way of dining. On the other hand, some of the textures and flavors will be strange to the diner who doesn't care to experiment.

A key to the Red Sea is injera, a very different form of bread, which arrives covering the bottom of a large tray to the depth of about a quarter inch. It has almost a fishnet look, and it's soft and spongy to the touch, tearing easily into smaller pieces. The taste is slightly sour, a result of fermentation taking place before baking, and I loved it. It's eaten with the fingers, and it's also a utensil; in other words, take a handful of injera, use it to grab some meat or vegetables, and eat.

Appetizers include a form of dumpling, like practically every other culture in the world, filled with either meat or vegetables. Entrees are stewed chicken or lamb, and a form of hamburger called kifto, eaten either raw or cooked, much like kibbee in

207

Middle Eastern restaurants. Meat tends to be tough and stringy, and most sauces have considerable spicing.

I liked the vegetables, which included red and green lentils, yellow split peas, stewed cabbage, and bulgar wheat, all cooked a long time. No broccoli or cauliflower, thank goodness.

RIDDLE'S PENULTIMATE CAFE
6307 Delmar Blvd.
(University City)
725-6985

Cuisine: Modern American, Cajun overtones
Serves: Dinner, Tuesday–Sunday; lunch, Tuesday–Friday
Prices: Moderate to expensive
Credit Cards: MC, V
Dress: Casual
Reservations: Accepted
Handicap Access: Satisfactory
Separate No-Smoking Section: No

They began in a diner-sized space near the University of Missouri–St. Louis in North County, serving wonderful pizza and pasta. They added a few special dishes here and there, saw their reputation grow, and in 1985, Andy and Paula Ayers moved to the University City Loop and opened Riddle's Penultimate.

The restaurant fits the eclectic, laid-back aura of the neighborhood, with a lot of mix-and-match furniture and a casual approach. But service is crisp and excellent, and Andy's cooking and Paula's baking have kept the restaurant at a high standard.

The Penultimate—Andy says he may have one more restaurant ahead—also boasts one of the city's best wine lists. Ayers was one of the first to offer a range of wine by the glass, changing his selections often. In addition to a fine cellar of imported and domestic wines, Ayers also has the largest Missouri selection in town. He is especially talented when it comes to creating dishes that are perfect matches for specific wines, and he can do it with beer, too.

There are Cajun touches to the menu, which has a wide range of appetizers and entrees, plus a handful of daily specials. Fowl and

209

fish of the season are used in abundance, and Ayers buys local produce whenever possible.

Stuffed mushrooms are a splendid appetizer, and so is chilled, grilled tenderloin with a tangy remoulade sauce. Soups are excellent; my favorite is a cream of chicken, enhanced by chunks of smoky ham. I'm not a fan of fruit soups—they're a little sweet for an early course—but Ayers made a believer of me with a tart, delicious apricot-orange, though I found it a better dessert.

If Riddle's has a signature dish, it's chicken Major Grey, with a tender, delicious breast in a ginger-chutney sauce that is perfect. Shrimp Sara involves a rich cream sauce with garlic and a hint of port. Steaks, with marchand de vin sauce on the side, are superior, as is grilled fresh fish.

Ayers' garlic potatoes are a must, by the way; I have friends who can make a meal of them. The sauce begins and ends with the generous use of garlic and includes lots of cream and butter.

Desserts are spectacular; fresh fruit pies lead the way, and there's homemade ice cream loaded with whatever happens to hit the Ayers' imagination, like bananas and macadamia nuts, or old-fashioned cinnamon red-hots.

ROYAL CHINESE B.B.Q.
8406 Olive Blvd.
(University City)
991-1888

❖❖

Cuisine: Chinese grills and barbecue
Serves: Lunch and dinner, every day
Prices: Moderate to expensive
Credit Cards: All major
Dress: Casual
Reservations: Accepted
Handicap Access: Passable (narrow entrance)
Separate No-Smoking Section: Yes

With ducks, geese, quail, and other fowl hanging in the window for all to ogle, and with cleaver-wielding cooks inside smiling as they hack birds, ribs, roast pork and other goodies into bite-sized pieces, the Royal Chinese B.B.Q. is the type of Chinese restaurant I've been waiting for in St. Louis since I first saw one in San Francisco too many years ago.

The small restaurant is bright enough to serve as a surgery, and the large Chinese menu on the wall makes me wonder what I'm missing—a situation that is not well resolved by a serving staff whose English is only a little better than my Chinese.

Oh, there's an English menu, with more than five dozen dishes on it, but I want to know more about "Buddhist Delight" and "Bubble Fried Scallops," and the difference between "Crispy Skin Roasted Pig" and "Chef's Special Roasted Pig," and my frustration builds.

Still, no matter what you get, or how you get it—by pointing at what's hanging in the kitchen or what is being enjoyed by the person at the next table—everything I've tried at the restaurant has been wonderful.

The Royal Chinese B.B.Q. is operated by the same people who also run my favorite dim sum spot, the China Royal, so they're two for two in terms of places to dine.

The menu here is very different; there are no appetizers in the traditional—maybe that's American traditional—style, like egg rolls or dumplings. Instead, there is congee, or rice soup, and noodles or rice noodles in soup. Then, the headings say, there are "Steamed or Simmered Specials," "Grilled Roasted Barbecue Style," "Seafood Specials," "Braised Noodles," and "Chow Mein" or "Chow Fun" (Hong Kong style).

My system has been to order three dishes for two adults, usually more than enough, and then to divide everything. The roast duck, under any prefix, has been crisp on the outside, juicy on the inside, and the ribs are tender and delicious.

Salt and pepper shrimp involves fresh, delicious shrimp stir-fried in their shells with lots of salt and pepper. They peel easily, and are simply delicious. Straw mushrooms with vegetables are a splendid dish, and noodles with duck a different delight. Barbecued quail is wonderful, and it would be worth the old Charles Lamb story about burning down the house to get roast pork so sweet and delicious.

SADIE THOMPSON'S
6347 North Rosebury Ave.
(Clayton)
863-4414

◆-◆

Cuisine: Continental
Serves: Dinner, Tuesday–Saturday; lunch, Tuesday–Friday
Prices: Moderate to expensive
Credit Cards: MC, V
Dress: Informal
Reservations: Accepted, usually required
Handicap Access: Satisfactory
Separate No-Smoking Section: Yes

Erv Janko began as a dessert-maker, and he sees desserts as a symbol of seduction. Ergo, he named his restaurant after one of the great sirens of literature and movies, Sadie Thompson. "And after all," he adds, "we are just across the street from a seminary."

Janko's middle-European delights first attracted the city's attention when he worked at the old Carpathia, a Hungarian restaurant on the South Side. His own place, with a kitchen that is largely open to view, is cheerful and friendly, with a choice of regular chairs or high stools.

The limited menu changes often but includes 4 or 5 entrees, hot and cold appetizers, and what he calls "meal-sized salads," which are exactly that. One of them, a sweet-and-sour salmon salad, is an exemplary dish. He grills a thick slice of marinated salmon and serves it, still warm, atop fresh greens, garnished with fruit and topped with a light teriyaki dressing. The combination is wonderful.

Janko's Hungarian background shows in the frequent use of fruit soups, including a delicious classic cherry. I think fruit soups splendid for summer, though I prefer the sweeter ones as desserts.

He also makes delightful pâtés, with his spicy seafood a real highlight.

Beef Wellington, long a personal favorite, comes out of Sadie's (or Erv's) kitchen in splendid style, close to rare enough, and with a nice topping of diced mushrooms between the beef and flaky brioche crust. A rich red wine sauce is a superior final fillip, and a good salad, and lightly cooked mixed fresh vegetables come alongside.

Baked sole stuffed with scallop mousse, and garlic-and-herb-seasoned chicken ragout, with tomatoes, onions, and bell peppers are two other good choices.

The wine list is modest but has some excellent matches for Janko's cooking, and he recommends some good ones on the menu.

Desserts vary wildly, according to the chef's mood, but they're all excellent. An apple-raisin pie, its crust fly-away light and flaky, was a wonder, and Key lime cheesecake is outstanding.

SALEEM'S

6501 Delmar Blvd.
(University City) **721-7947**

20 Clarkson Center
(Chesterfield) **530-9010**

❖❖❖

Cuisine: Lebanese
Serves: Dinner, Monday–Saturday
Prices: Inexpensive to moderate
Credit Cards: MC, V
Dress: Casual
Reservations: Accepted
Handicap Access: Satisfactory
Separate No-Smoking Section: No

Salim Hanna has expanded the dining boundaries of St. Louisans in several ways—first with excellent Lebanese cuisine and then, especially pleasing to me, by popularizing that most-maligned delicacy, garlic.

Hanna, who deliberately misspelled his first name to help Americans pronounce it, has garlic festivals a few times a year, when the misnamed "stinking weed" becomes king. He also prepares roast garlic as a regular item, and when it's well cooked, the garlic cloves have just a hint of the wonderful flavor and not its power.

Primarily, Saleem's is for Lebanese cooking—for that whole array of marvelous appetizers built around eggplant, chick peas, and fava beans. The eggplant dip, creamy and garlicky, with a tang of lemon, is delicious, and so is hummus, or mashed chick peas with garlic, sesame, and lemon; or tabuli, a blend of whole wheat and parsley.

Shish kebabs are splendid; both beef and lamb are nicely marinated before skewering and grilling. A delightful dish one evening was a catfish, not battered and fried in the usual manner, but spiced and grilled. Delicious.

There's a limited wine list and traditional, sweet desserts like baklava and halvah, plus strong, dark coffee as the perfect accompaniment.

The second location, new in 1991, is smaller and deep in the far west county, operated by a relative, but under Salim Hanna's supervision.

SEKI'S JAPANESE RESTAURANT
6335 Delmar Blvd.
(University City)
726-6477

Cuisine: Japanese
Serves: Lunch and dinner, Monday–Saturday
Prices: Moderate
Credit Cards: All major
Dress: Informal
Reservations: Accepted
Handicap Access: Satisfactory
Separate No-Smoking Section: Yes

The arrival of a Japanese restaurant to the University City Loop just about fills the ethnic parade—American, Lebanese, Chinese, French-ish, Pakistani, Thai, Mexican, Italian, Ethiopian, Korean—which makes the neighborhood so exciting.

Seki's Japanese Restaurant came with 1992 and shows signs of being a welcome addition.

Small and brightly lighted, Seki's has a sushi bar that affects my adult inhibitions the way penny-candy displays did in my childhood. I can sit in front of it for hours, watching the chef work and ordering one of these and two of those until my stomach is full and my wallet empty. Tuna, salmon, yellowtail, mackerel, sea urchin, squid, octopus, giant clam, salmon caviar, and others just make my appetite perk up, especially when the chef places them atop a chunk of chilled rice that has been touched with a little—just a little, please—of that fiery green horseradish.

A marinated jellyfish appetizer was tasty, though its texture was slightly off-putting, the bean soup is splendid, and tempura is always a winner.

TED AND TEIKO'S
9937 Manchester Road
(Warson Woods)
961-1933

‹›

Cuisine: Japanese at dinner, general at lunch
Serves: Dinner, Monday–Saturday; lunch, Monday–Friday
Prices: Moderate
Credit Cards: MC, V
Dress: Informal
Reservations: Accepted for dinner
Handicap Access: Satisfactory
Separate No-Smoking Section: Yes

If a restaurant can be described as schizophrenic, that's the way to classify Ted and Teiko's. A small, popular spot in a Warson Woods strip shopping center, it offers standard lunch fare—with an Asiatic touch here and there—from a steam table, but once the sun goes over the yardarm, it becomes a Japanese restaurant.

It even makes Kipling's twain have a meeting; at lunch one can have sushi and an egg-salad sandwich, or won ton soup preceding Italian-style pasta or a cheeseburger.

Given my predilection for sushi, I always find it a superior appetizer, but the won ton soup is a winner, too.

The dinner selection also includes excellent shrimp and vegetable tempura; steaks and fish with teriyaki sauce; and sukiyaki, with beef and vegetables cooked together in soy sauce and meat broth.

218

THAI CAFE
6170 Delmar Blvd.
862-6868

‡‡

Cuisine: Thai
Serves: Dinner, Monday–Saturday; lunch, Monday–Friday
Prices: Inexpensive to moderate
Credit Cards: All major
Dress: Informal
Reservations: Accepted
Handicap Access: Satisfactory
Separate No-Smoking Area: Yes

From the first step inside to the final departure, the word *delicate* keeps coming to mind at the Thai Cafe. The walls, the decorations, the attitude of the servers, and the meals all fit that word. The restaurant, opened late in 1991, is a splendid addition to the city.

It's a few doors east of Skinker Boulevard, and about a block outside the University City Loop, but it fits so well into the ethnic mix of that neighborhood that it would be unfeeling to place it anywhere else.

There are hot-and-spicy dishes, and mild ones, dishes served atop mounds of noodles or wrapped in cool lettuce leaves, dishes with the pop of chilies or lemon grass or coriander, or the tang of lime juice or the fire of curry. Everything has been splendid.

Spring rolls, known here as crispy rolls, are exactly that, with ground pork, shrimp, and garlic bringing a pleasing flavor. Thai sticks, which involve a shrimp wrapped in ground pork, then battered and fried, are a treat, and so is satay, with marinated chicken or pork skewered and grilled, served with a spicy peanut sauce.

Stir-fried dishes offer chicken, pork, beef, or shrimp, or no meat at all, cooked with a variety of spices and vegetables. Pad gra ree, flavorful and piquant, adds curry powder, onions, and both hot and sweet peppers.

Different curry combinations bring different flavors, and different amounts of fire. And the dishes are available with or without meat. Red curry, with basil leaves, does some wonderful things to shrimp. Noodles, either soft or fried, are the base for many dishes.

Service is friendly, and the Thai Cafe provides dishes with their own personality. Adding the personality of the chefs is the sort of nifty thing that sets one restaurant apart from another and makes all of them necessary to a community.

WEBSTER GRILL & CAFE
8127 Big Bend Blvd.
(Webster Groves)
962-0564

❖◆◆◆❖

Cuisine: Modern American, also vegetarian dishes
Serves: Dinner, every day; lunch, Monday–Saturday; brunch, Saturday–Sunday
Prices: Moderate
Credit Cards: All major
Dress: Casual
Reservations: Accepted
Handicap Access: Entrance satisfactory, rest rooms very difficult (stairs)
Separate No-Smoking Section: No

Like a lot of people who grew up in the '60s but changed lifestyle in the 1980s, the Webster Grill & Cafe moved to new quarters, redecorated, went upscale with its menu—and lost some of its charm.

The primarily stir-fried and vegetarian cooking style vanished in favor of modern American; white tablecloths bloomed, and the mix-and-match decor disappeared. The Repertory Theatre of St. Louis and Webster University are nearby, so the friendly, casual attitude remains.

A major improvement is a larger, more interesting wine list, with some good values and creative pairings with entrees. There are Southwestern overtones to many of the meals, and some good pasta dishes, like the fettucine with four cheeses—fontina, gorgonzola, cheddar, and Parmesan—and linguine with vegetables.

Sautéd trout is a superior dish, as are grilled chicken breast with black beans and grilled shrimp with a citrus and olive oil marinade.

Soups are tasty, and both the spinach and the Caesar salads are excellent lunchtime meals. Desserts are standard.

THE WISHING WELL
8435 Airport Rd.
(Berkeley)
521-8743

•••

Cuisine: American
Serves: Lunch and dinner, Tuesday–Saturday
Prices: Inexpensive to moderate
Credit Cards: All major
Dress: Informal
Reservations: Accepted
Handicap Access: Satisfactory
Separate No-Smoking Section: No

The Wishing Well, in the North County, not far from Lambert Field, sometimes seems to be a restaurant frozen in amber. I've been visiting it for the 20 years I've been writing about restaurants, and it never seems to change.

Meals are reasonably priced and well prepared, and there are such old-fashioned touches as a choice among five different potatoes, filet mignon that is wrapped in bacon, turtle soup as a regular entry, catfish that is served whole, with both ends flopping over the edges of the plate, anchovies in the Caesar salad, and an appetizer list that includes "Angels on Horseback."

Once a popular hors d'oeuvre, angels on horseback, or chicken livers wrapped in bacon, have become almost extinct in these health-conscious days. But they still taste good, and the Wishing Well's were extra-good because the livers were tender and juicy, and the bacon properly crisp.

There are Italian overtones to many of the veal dishes, and pasta is available as a side dish. Salad or soup, plus potato, pasta, or vegetable, accompany all entrees, which keeps prices modest, and an extra $1.50 for a Caesar salad qualifies as a bargain.

The Wishing Well provides a catfish that is among the very best in town—good-sized, with a proper cornmeal crust and fried to the perfect moment, when the outside is crisp and tasty, and the fish flaky with the wonderful, rich flavor that a good catfish will display.

Veal dishes are satisfactory, steaks better, and a side order of thin pasta with butter, garlic, and anchovies is a spectacular dish, but only if your companions for the ride home are close friends.

Homemade cheesecake, rich and smooth, is a proper dessert.

ZINNIA
7491 Big Bend Blvd.
(Webster Groves)
962-0572

Cuisine: Modern American
Serves: Dinner, Tuesday–Sunday; lunch, Monday–Friday
Prices: Moderate to expensive
Credit Cards: MC, V
Dress: Informal
Reservations: Accepted (advised on weekends)
Handicap Access: Satisfactory
Separate No-Smoking Section: No

Like most of St. Louis's successful restaurateurs, David Guempel began in someone else's kitchen. He was the executive chef at Balaban's before moving to Webster Groves three years ago and opening Zinnia, a small, charming restaurant with exemplary food.

Guempel is one of the city's most talented chefs, a man who cooks with style and grace and, even more important, imagination and love. He understands that a light hand is needed with herbs and spices, and he uses them to complement dishes in superior manner. He also knows the appetizing effect of presentation, and each dish at Zinnia is a beautiful creation.

The menu changes seasonally and is bolstered by a fish, a pasta, and a soup of the day, plus a couple of specials. Home-smoked meats are regular items, and an early signature dish was a smoked, grilled leg of lamb that was as good a lamb as I've ever had—flavorful and fork-tender.

Appetizers are led by marvelous mussels, poached and served chilled with a honey-dill sauce that brightens the taste buds. Homemade pâté is a brilliantly blended mousse of chicken, turkey, and pork livers, heightened by a hint of truffles; and sesame lamb meatballs have a touch of the exotic Middle East. Baby pork back ribs, grilled in a honey-soy sauce, also sparkle.

Trout Zinnia is topped with a light crust of sesame seeds, pine nuts, and pecans, bringing a superb set of flavors, and soft-shell crabs, always a delicacy, are made even better by Guempel's flash-frying, which makes them melt-in-the mouth tender.

Persian lamb kebabs, grilled and served with a delicate fruit sauce, deserve high marks and so do the sweetbreads, prepared to the chef's mood of the day. They are always exceptional.

Desserts vary with the fruit of the season, or the day, but again Guempel shows a winning touch. Strawberry shortcake, with tender berries on a flaky biscuit, topped with fresh whipped cream, is a classic dessert prepared in a classic style.

ZORBA'S

6346 Delmar Blvd.
(University City) **721-5638**

39 North Central Ave.
(Clayton) **727-4976**

8143 Big Bend Blvd.
(Webster Groves) **968-6818**

◆◆

Cuisine: Greek
Serves: Lunch and dinner, Monday–Saturday
Prices: Inexpensive
Credit Cards: None
Dress: Casual
Reservations: Not applicable
Handicap Access: Satisfactory
Separate No-Smoking Section: No

These small, storefront operations began in the University City
Loop and, after setting a firm foundation for good, simple, Greek
food, nicely prepared and modestly priced, have spread through
the Mid-County area, with recent additions in Clayton and
Webster Groves.

Zorba's is more for lunch or a quick meal than for real dining,
though there are plans for a white tablecloth dining room in
Clayton, but it provides some of the better simple Greek cooking
in town, especially the gyro sandwiches, which seem fresher and
tastier than others I've sampled.

Hummus, and cheese and spinach pie are splendid, and salads
are crisp and heavy with feta cheese.

Lamb and chicken kebabs are grilled to order, and the dolmathes, or stuffed grape leaves, are excellent. So are a couple of
my Greek favorites, the casserole-style moussaka and pasticcio.

226

The former involves ground beef and eggplant, the latter ground beef, macaroni, and cheese, almost like a Greek lasagna. Desserts are sweet and delightful.

There's nothing formal about Zorba's, but it fills a need and is one of my favorite lunch stops. And afterward, I almost feel like singing and dancing like its namesake.

WEST COUNTY

Lindbergh Boulevard and beyond, with Highway 40 as the dividing line between north and south.

Agostino's Colosseum (north)
Annie Gunn's (south)
AOI (south)
Benedetto's (south)
Bentley's Restaurant and Pub (south)
Brett Hull's Restaurant & Grill (north)
Bristol Bar & Grill (north)
Cafe Renee (south)
Casa Gallardo (north)
China Royal (north)
Dierdorf & Hart's (north, see Downtown listings)
Elsah Landing Restaurant (south)
Forbidden City (south)
G. P. Agostino's (south, see Agostino's Colosseum, above)
Giovanni's Little Place (south, see Giovanni's in South listings)
Hunan and Peking Garden (south)
Jeremiah's (south)
John Mineo's (south)
Kreis' (north)
Massa's Restaurant (2 north, 2 south)
Pacific Shore Cafe (north)
Patrick's (1 north, 1 south)
Pueblo Nuevo (north)
Robata of Japan (north)
S & P Oyster Co. (south)
Tachibana (north)
Tutto Bene (south, see LoRusso's, South listings)
The Village Bar (south)

AGOSTINO'S COLOSSEUM
12949 Olive Blvd. (at Fee Fee Rd.) 434-2959

G. P. AGOSTINO'S
15846 Manchester Rd. (at Clarkson) 391-5480

Cuisine: Italian
Serves: Agostino's Colosseum: dinner, Monday–Saturday;
G. P. Agostino's: dinner, every day; lunch, Monday–Friday
Prices: Expensive
Credit Cards: All major
Dress: Informal
Reservations: Accepted
Handicap Access: Satisfactory
Separate No-Smoking Section: No

Agostino's was one of the first of the city's top-drawer Italian restaurants to leave the Hill in favor of a West County location. Not only has it remained a leader, but it has spun off a second establishment for a second generation.

The fare is hearty and of southern Italian heritage, like most St. Louis Italian restaurants, with large portions and a loving, generous touch with garlic in many dishes.

While the Colosseum hides considerable elegance behind a plain storefront in a strip shopping center, G. P.'s is a free-standing building with columns in front and a rich, plush interior. Black tie is the order of the day for serving personnel at both.

Pastas are made fresh with rich sauces; green noodles with clams are a longtime specialty, or are prepared with pesto sauce in spectacular manner. Most pastas are available either as appetizers or entrees. There's also a splendid touch with squid; my favorite appetizer brings it sautéd lightly with fresh tomatoes, lemon, and a hint of garlic. The cheese-garlic bread is wonderful but extremely filling.

Beef tenderloin, sliced and served with a superior Bordelaise sauce, is an outstanding entree, and Agostino's does some outstanding things with top-quality veal, too. Steamed fresh spinach usually is available as a side dish, topped with a handful of sweet, red peppers for color, texture, and flavor.

Some good Italian entrees head the wine list, and the cannoli is a perfect dessert.

ANNIE GUNN'S
16806 Chesterfield Airport Rd.
(West of Chesterfield Mall)
532-7684

Cuisine: American
Serves: Lunch and dinner, Tuesday–Sunday
Prices: Moderate to expensive
Credit Cards: MC, V
Dress: Casual
Reservations: Accepted
Handicap Access: Satisfactory
Separate No-Smoking Section: No

Next door to Tom and Jane Sehnert's Smoke House, one of the great food purveyors in the area, stood the Pot Roast Inn, a grubby old bar with a marvelous name. They took it over, remodeled it, stocked it from their shop, and opened it as a superb bar-restaurant, named in honor of Tom's Irish grandmother.

The menu is simple, with steaks, chops, and fresh fish, plus gigantic, matchless sandwiches for either lunch or dinner. Appetizers run the usual gamut, but the top of the line is the smoked trout, made next door and supplied to many of the city's best restaurants. Chicken wings are good, and potato skins are tasty and very filling. Homemade potato soup is a perfect winter warmer, and the addition of the market's smoked bacon adds a delightful fillip of extra flavor.

Sirloins and filets head the steaks, and chicken breasts are prepared in various ways, but the smoked pork chops, also from the market, are something very special.

Smoked turkey and bratwurst are superior sandwiches, and the house bacon makes a classic BLT in a super-classic manner.

Braunschweiger and thinly sliced onion on rye deserves plaudits, too.

Annie Gunn's is a winner in every respect, but go next door to grocery shop *after* eating.

AOI
902 Town & Country Commons
(Clayton and Woods Mill Roads)
394-3114

❖❖❖

Cuisine: Japanese
Serves: Dinner, Tuesday–Sunday; lunch, Wednesday–Friday
Prices: Moderate
Credit Cards: All major
Dress: Informal
Reservations: Accepted
Handicap Access: Satisfactory
Separate No-Smoking Section: No smoking in restaurant

Sleek and simple to the point of being stark, AOI—pronounced "OW-ee"—brings excellent Japanese cuisine to the West County, with a collection of glorious appetizers, nicely prepared entrees, and an interesting gimmick of cooking tableside on hot rocks.

No, not stolen jewels, but porous gray stones that are heated in a pizza oven, then carried (very carefully) to tableside. The waiter cuts chunks of beef, for example, from a large steak, places them on the rock, and watches them cook. It's dry cooking, and the porous stone supposedly absorbs the grease. In any event, the beef was tender and tasty, and a soy-based dipping sauce added some extra flavor.

The AOI appetizers are some of the best I've tried, led by fried oysters that are exceptional. They taste as if they've just been opened, rolled in bread crumbs, and fried quickly. The result is sweet, juicy, tender oysters that are bursting with flavor.

Both sushi (raw fish on slightly vinegary, cold rice with a tiny bit of torrid green horseradish) and sashimi (raw fish in thin slices with rice and horseradish on the side) are elegant and, in Japanese style, beautifully displayed on the plate. Marinated meat, fish, and vegetables, skewered and grilled over an open flame, are perfectly cooked and splendid.

The hot stones also work wonders with scallops and shrimp, adding a quick char so that the edges are crisp and the insides succulently soft. And for a bean-curd lover like me, the sautéd tofu was another winner. Both chicken broth and bean soup are light and tasty.

Entrees include glorious, cloud-light tempura (also available as an appetizer) that makes fried food a sensual experience and not just dinner. There's also the steak grilled on the stone, and some fish items that were less satisfactory.

The classic sukiyaki, beef and vegetables cooked in delicious broth at the table, was most proper. The beef, beautiful and very thinly sliced, comes on a separate plate and the diner takes a few slices, tosses them into the broth-and-vegetable filled pot, watches them cook for a minute or two (or longer), removes them, along with a few noodles, some bean curd, and vegetables, eats, and repeats the process until the beef is gone and the diner is full.

AOI also boasts a wide variety of saki, some to be served hot, some cold. I'd never tried the cold saki before, and it was okay, but I prefer Japanese beer with a Japanese meal.

BENEDETTO'S
12240 Manchester Rd.
Colonnade Shopping Center
(East of Ballas Rd.)
821-2555

Cuisine: Italian
Serves: Dinner, Tuesday–Sunday; lunch, Tuesday–Friday
Prices: Moderate to expensive
Credit Cards: All major
Dress: Informal
Reservations: Accepted
Handicap Access: Satisfactory
Separate No-Smoking Section: Yes

While less deserving restaurants sometimes get more public praise, Benedetto Buzzeta and his wife, Lia, continue to provide meals as good, and as elegant, as any in the area.

Buzzetta is a modest man; he originally called his restaurant the Brother-in-Law's, paying homage to his relative, restaurateur John Mineo, but also putting himself in an undeserved shadow. The name later was changed but, thankfully, nothing else, with superior meals coming from a modest location in the West County.

The strongly southern Italian menu has similarities with many of the other fine Italian restaurants in the city, but there are always some lovely individual touches that show the Benedetto stamp.

Porcini mushrooms do wonderful things to excellent risotto, with the long grains of Italian rice perfectly prepared with olive oil and saffron. Snails have a hint of fennel in the sauce, and fresh tomatoes top a cannelloni appetizer, which has a superior stuffing. Seafood salad, with squid, shrimp, and scallops, has a tangy dressing that brings hints of ceviche.

Buzzetta also does exciting things with his marinara sauce; it's

236

dark and and full-flavored, with just enough garlic and superior black olive flavor. It's available with several different dishes; the baby squid is my favorite.

Artichoke hearts and mushrooms make a rich, hearty sauce for delicious, fork-tender veal, and so does prosciutto and cheese. The classic veal chop is cooked to perfection, and veal tenderloin, with sherry, mushrooms, and capers, also shows the Benedetto touch with flavors that blend perfectly. Beef tenderloin, with mushrooms, tomatoes, and Marsala wine, is fork-tender and delicious, and the same cut, broiled with lots of lemon and garlic, is as good a steak as I know.

Steamed fresh spinach, served with diced pimentos on top and a hint of vinegar, is a special vegetable, while pasta is outstanding, too, either as an entree or an appetizer. A simple dish of thin spaghetti with olive oil and garlic is a classic.

The dining area has a softly lighted elegance that provides comfort and relaxation. Service is good, and dinner is improved by a well-rounded wine list that has many solid Italian and California selections.

The dessert cart looks rich and delicious, and a Napoleon-style chocolate cake is a winner.

BENTLEY'S RESTAURANT AND PUB
11915 Manchester Road
821-5515

✦-✦

Cuisine: American
Serves: Dinner, every day; brunch, Sunday
Prices: Moderate to expensive
Credit Cards: All major
Dress: Informal
Reservations: Accepted
Handicap Access: Satisfactory
Separate No-Smoking Section: Yes

Good prime rib has become more and more difficult to find in American restaurants, so it's a pleasure to have places like Bentley's in the neighborhood.

The veteran St. Louis establishment has specialized in prime rib for many years and has always delivered properly. In addition, it offers well-prepared, moderately priced American fare. The highly satisfactory steaks, chops, and seafood specialities are served in comfortable rooms complete with fireplaces.

It's nothing fancy but is guaranteed to satisfy the desire for good beef. Dinner also includes pleasant salads, adequate vegetables, and a nice array of desserts.

BRETT HULL'S RESTAURANT & GRILL

100 Four Seasons Shopping Center (Olive Boulevard at Woods Mill Road)

878-0909

❖—❖

Cuisine: Modern American, Southwestern
Serves: Dinner every day; lunch, Monday–Saturday
Prices: Inexpensive to moderate
Credit Cards: All major
Dress: Informal
Reservations: Not accepted
Handicap Access: Satisfactory
Separate No-Smoking Section: Yes

The new Brett Hull's Restaurant and Grill is not only a splendid example of a menu for "grazing," but also a fascinating look at the corporate thinking of the Pasta House Company—the city's most successful restaurant chain. In addition, it is probably the most interesting restaurant to open here in the past year.

It's doubtful that Brett Hull cooks any better than chef Steve Goodwin plays hockey, but the Blues' scoring machine has loaned (or leased) his name to an establishment that blends all the ingredients of Modern American cuisine in exemplary fashion.

Those consistent Italian favorites, pizza and pasta, make a strong appearance, but there are also dishes representing the Far East, Mexico, Southwestern America, and traditional America. But there's mix-and-match there, too, with a Cajun sauce on pasta, pesto sauce with Chinese dumplings, lime sour cream on smoked duck quesadillas, Chinese salsa on grilled tuna, pasta with lamb sausage and feta cheese, and old favorites like pot roast, or meat loaf with mashed potatoes.

239

Hull's is a Pasta House operation but unlike any other restaurant in the chain. Instead of specializing in satisfactory, inexpensive, rather bland pasta served in large amounts, Brett Hull's may be a positive sign for the future.

Goodwin, who came from California to join the corporation, is a chef with considerable imagination and a generous hand with herbs and spices. The Cajun sauce on the pasta, for example, has a wonderful pop.

The menu is divided into sections labeled appetizers, salads, pasta, pizza, and entrees, with prices and portions that encourage one from each department to create a full meal, especially if you add dessert.

Occasionally, imagination outdoes execution. The pesto sauce on dumplings was garlicky and delicious, but the dumplings themselves fell short. Baked Brie didn't make it, but the roasted garlic and tomato chutney served alongside were brilliantly prepared. Crab cakes, crisp on the outside, soft within, were helped by a chili pepper–bolstered tartar sauce. Soft, tasty quesadillas were topped with rich, well-smoked duck for a splendid combination.

Tuna, rare in the middle and charred on the edges, was nicely complemented by the ginger-rich Chinese salsa, and smoked chicken, rubbed with herbs and lemon before a light grilling, was sweet and juicy. Seasonal vegetables accompany all entrees.

Pizza has worldwide toppings, like Thai chicken with peanut sauce, barbecued chicken, smoked salmon, and duck sausage, as well as the traditional pepperoni, eggplant, mozzarella cheese, and Italian sausage. The crust is a little thick for my taste, but it's fresh and tasty.

The wine list is another plus; it is limited, but almost all the bottles are under $20, and there are some pleasant and worthy selections that go well with the fare.

Desserts vary, but a blueberry-peach crisp is fruity and outstanding, with a crackly crust and some honey ice cream on top to add the ultimate accent. Crême brulée, offered one night, suffered from a too-thick custard.

Service is brisk and friendly, the room slightly loud with lots of television sets tuned to sports events and hockey memorabilia everywhere. But after all, it is named for a hockey star—and a gift shop offers jerseys, pictures, and even hockey pucks to take home.

BRISTOL BAR & GRILL
11801 Olive Blvd.
(At Ballas)
567-0272

❖❖❖

Cuisine: Seafood, Modern American
Serves: Lunch and Dinner, every day; brunch on Sunday
Prices: Moderate to expensive
Credit Cards: All major
Dress: Informal
Reservations: Accepted
Handicap Access: Satisfactory
Separate No-Smoking Section: Yes

A decade or so ago, when air freight came into its own and fresh seafood began arriving daily in St. Louis and other midwestern cities, the Bristol Bar & Grill helped us to move out of the doldrums of shrimp, filet of so-called sole, and catfish— all fried—that passed for the seafood selection in most restaurants.

A stylish chain operation, the Bristol also introduced the open-kitchen concept, and watching the cooks work is still a pleasure. The restaurant, larger than it looks but still offering the illusion of pleasant smallness, provides fine service and generally good meals, improved by fresh biscuits that always arrive at the table just as the current ones are being finished.

The seafood variety, depending on the season, is usually excellent, fresh, and nicely prepared. There are occasional flashes of inconsistency, and dishes tend to be on the bland side, perhaps aimed at the lowest common dining denominator.

A nice touch is the wide variety of fresh oysters, depending on availability. That plus was offset one night by a waiter who offered "Rockpoint oysters": when I asked for a more specific home, I was told they came from Rockpoint.

"Well, where is Rockpoint?" I asked. "Is it Long Island, or Maine, or the Chesapeake Bay?"

"Yes," was the reply, "up there somewhere, in the Northeastern part."

They turned out to be from Long Island, were more commonly known as Blue Points, and were delicious.

Oysters Rockefeller are topped with cheese, which doesn't belong, but oysters themselves are excellent, and fried calimari is outstanding.

Soft fish like grouper and bluefish can be excellent, and I think bluefish, just broiled, is as good a fish as the ocean offers. Norwegian salmon, perfectly grilled, is delicious, its delicate flavor coming through nicely.

Vegetables come alongside. Boiled potatoes and cole slaw are my favorites. Yams under a walnut sauce are fine, if you like 'em sweet. But pasta is overdone and tasteless.

The wine list is long and excellent, with a splendid selection of California whites.

Desserts include pies and cheesecakes of various types, and they're usually satisfactory.

243

CAFE RENEE
403 Lafayette Center
(Manchester at Baxter Road)
394-6445

❖❖

Cuisine: American Modern, French overtones
Serves: Lunch and dinner, Monday–Saturday
Prices: Inexpensive to moderate
Credit Cards: MC, V
Dress: Informal
Reservations: Accepted
Handicap Access: Satisfactory
Separate No-Smoking Section: No

Cafe Renee may offer as worldwide a selection of food as any restaurant in the area. Most of the recipes seem to be of French origin, though there are some from Belgium. These fine European foundations are then touched with herbs and spices of the Far East, or something as basically American as bourbon and pecans.

The results are some magical dishes turned out of a tiny kitchen tucked away in a West County shopping center. The menu is limited but there is an extensive use of fresh, seasonal meats and produce, plus a fresh fish and a pasta of the day. There are occasional special menus, and I got lucky one night to find a Holland-Belgium festival that included two of my favorite dishes: fresh herring and mussels steamed in the Belgian style, with lots of onions and leeks.

Everything is very tasty, and the modest prices make Cafe Renee a real bargain.

Soups are outstanding, with a French onion in the classic style, rich with cheese, and a split pea that is thick and flavorful, helped by sizable chunks of smoky ham. Salads are delicious, with a properly garlicky house dressing and delicious, crunchy croutons made on the premises.

Entrees are eminently satisfactory. Fettuccine with clams, mussels, and shrimp is delicious, made extraordinary by a hint of curry and the fact that both clams and mussels are cooked and served in the shells, allowing their juices to improve everything.

Beef tenderloin medallions with artichokes, tomatoes, and mushrooms are an equally superior dish, exemplifying simple fare prepared in a careful and imaginative manner. The pork tenderloin, in a honey glaze, is a little sweet for my taste, but the use of both dark and white raisins made for a lovely presentation. Grilled salmon, with a superb dill sauce, was cooked to the perfect moment.

Vegetables show the same care.

The wine list is small, but with some nice accompaniments at moderate prices. Desserts are delightful, displaying the same philosophy that simple dishes, well prepared, will do the job. For example, an old-fashioned pineapple upside-down cake, something I haven't seen on a menu in years, was offered one night; it was perfect. Cream puffs are almost an out-of-body experience.

CASA GALLARDO
462 West Port Plaza
(I-270 and Page Boulevard)
434-7755

❖❖

Cuisine: Mexican
Serves: Dinner, every day; Lunch, Monday–Saturday
Prices: Moderate
Credit Cards: All major
Dress: Casual
Reservations: Accepted
Handicap Access: Satisfactory
Separate No-Smoking Section: Yes

When Ramon Gallardo opened the first Mexican restaurant to bear his name in the then-new West Port Plaza area, he brought a splendid dining experience to the city. At the same time, he achieved a dream that began as he was still a dishwasher and grew through many years in the restaurant business.

Success was immediate, and a major chain showed major interest. Expansion followed, Gallardo became wealthy, and the food at the restaurants grew more and more bland. He soon withdrew, went into other restaurant operations, and is planning a new Mexican-Southwestern restaurant to open in 1992, if economic conditions permit.

The restaurants remain popular, but I find the meals of little flavor. When another West County location served me plain ketchup and called it salsa, I decided I'd had enough.

Note that there are eight Casa Gallardo restaurants in the area, all with similar menus, prices, food, and service. This was the first one.

246

CHINA ROYAL
5911 North Lindbergh
(At Brown Road and
McDonnell Boulevard)
731-1313

❖❖

Cuisine: Chinese, with dim sum at lunch and on Sunday
Serves: Lunch and dinner, every day
Prices: Inexpensive to moderate
Credit Cards: All major
Dress: Casual
Reservations: Accepted
Handicap Access: Satisfactory
Separate No-Smoking Section: Yes

Until the early '70s, Chinese food in St. Louis was Cantonese-American, and there wasn't much of it worth writing home about. Then the Hunan-Szechuan Revolution brought the spicy dishes of northern China, and the city soon had almost as much Chinese cuisine as it did Italian.

For a while, there were a lot of "hot" Chinese restaurants, but they came and went. Today, after a lengthy shakedown voyage, the China Royal has come forth as the leader in several ways. It serves the best dim sum in the area, its regular menu is sometimes just as good, and it is the parent of the Royal Chinese Barbecue (see Mid-County section), offering different, delightful dishes that no one else can match.

In a building that once housed a fast-food operation, China Royal now has all the classic decorative overtones, including many lanterns and a large tank of gorgeous fish. The Sunday dim sum has become so popular that people start lining up before the 11 o'clock opening bell; the crowd is mainly Asiatic.

Dim sum is available for lunch on other days too, but on Sunday the selection is largest and the dishes freshest.

There's also a regular menu at lunch and dinner, and it's very good.

Dim sum is like a traveling buffet. Waiters push carts to the tables, describe the dishes they carry and serve what you want. Portions are not quite as large as regular appetizers, but a serving is usually just right for two to have a good taste, and the cart will be back with more in a little while.

The list is almost endless, including a variety of dumplings, shrimp, and fish in several sauces, roast pork, ribs, chicken, and more traditional Chinese fare like tripe, stewed duck feet in hot sauce, and noodles. Dessert carts arrive later, piled high with Chinese pastries, and rice and tea come alongside. When it's all over, one pays by the plate.

A party of four can eat for several hours, and that seems to be the style at dim sum—leisurely meals, lots of conversation, and a wide variety of different tastes. I love it, and the offerings at China Royal match those I've tried in other cities.

Dinner is almost as good, with a number of dishes that are not seen on every Chinese menu in town, and the added delight of having Peking duck available without the necessity of ordering a day or two in advance. One duck easily serves four people—it's expensive, and there's a 45-minute wait, but diners can relax over a drink and a couple of appetizers before it arrives. Its flavor is smoky and wonderful, but the skin has been inconsistent in terms of crispness, and the rice pancakes are not always hot enough.

The menu has the usual asterisks to indicate hot and spicy dishes, but I've had to ask for extra-hot in order to get them not fiery, but properly tangy, and too often the chef has merely tossed some extra peppers onto the dish, which does nothing to relieve blandness unless you bite into one, at which point it's far too hot. I hope the same creeping blandness that has affected many Mexican restaurants in the city is not contagious.

Egg rolls are spectacular, with some delicate spicing not tasted very often, and spare ribs are smoky, meaty, and delicious. Crab

Rangoon displays a too-tough skin and hot and sour soup isn't peppery enough.

Szechuan chicken pot is much like Jewish chicken in the pot, but without the matzo balls. It's bland, but the chicken and vegetables and rich stock are delicious. Beef with four flavors— pepper, garlic, ginger, and green onions—was very good, and would have been superb if the beef itself had been less tough.

Shrimp and pork, Peking style, involves shrimp in a red sauce and pork in black bean sauce. They're oddly complementary, and the dish is delicious.

There's a small wine list but also some imported beer, and I prefer Chinese beer with Chinese food. Fortune cookies—and the fortunes—haven't changed through the centuries.

DIERDORF & HART'S

West Port Plaza, I-270 and Page 878-1801
Union Station 421-1772

Cuisine: Steaks, chops, and seafood
Serves: Lunch and dinner, every day
Prices: Expensive, sometimes very expensive
Credit Cards: All major
Dress: Informal
Reservations: Accepted
Handicap Access: Satisfactory
Separate No-Smoking Section: Yes

The West Port Plaza location was the first place the two former football Cardinals entered the restaurant business. Menu, service, prices, cuisine, and shortcomings are very similar to the Union Station location discussed in the Downtown section.

ELSAH LANDING RESTAURANT

Plaza Frontenac 432-8055

Lindbergh and Clayton Roads
Alton, IL 618-374-1607

Cuisine: American, features desserts
Serves: Lunch and dinner, every day
Prices: Inexpensive to moderate
Credit Cards: Not accepted
Dress: Informal
Reservations: None at Plaza Frontenac, lunch and tea only in Alton
Handicap Access: Satisfactory
Separate No-Smoking Section: No smoking in either restaurant

If you build a better mousetrap, or bake a better pie, the world will beat a path to your door. The Landing began as a lunch, dessert, and tea room looking out on the Mississippi River and the Great River Road in Alton, Illinois.

Word spread, as word does, and soon everyone wanted some of the brilliant fruit pies and other desserts, bringing about a second location established in the Plaza Frontenac shopping center, cheek by jowl with Neiman-Marcus and Saks Fifth Avenue.

The suburban Landing serves excellent soups, good sandwiches, and superlative desserts, just as it does at the Illinois location—which is farther from the city, but offers a much better view.

FORBIDDEN CITY
1 Nationalway Center
(Woods Mill at Manchester Rd.)
394-8008

Cuisine: Chinese
Serves: Lunch and dinner, every day
Prices: Inexpensive to moderate
Credit Cards: All major
Dress: Informal
Reservations: Accepted
Handicap Access: Satisfactory
Separate No-Smoking Section: Yes

Northern Chinese cuisine, featuring the spicy foods of Hunan, Peking (now Beijing), and Szechuan, has become the standard in St. Louis. Too many menus appear identical, but here and there, a devoted diner can find a restaurant that brings a few additional touches that set it above the rest.

Sometimes the touches are as simple as higher-quality ingredients that are freshly prepared, and that seems to be the secret at Forbidden City.

A classically simple dish, one I remember from childhood visits to Chinese restaurants, is Cantonese-style shrimp in lobster sauce. In those days, when lobster was less expensive, it was Cantonese-style lobster, but in the same delicious sauce with garlic, mushrooms, eggs, peas, bamboo shoots, and scallions. Forbidden City does it brilliantly.

Braised eggplant, nicely spiced, is a rich vegetarian dish, and pork yu-shung, with water chestnuts, mushrooms, and lots of spicing, is fresh and very tasty.

Egg rolls, fat and rich, are a traditional and well-prepared appetizer, as are pot-stickers, nicely crisp on one side. Soups also are outstanding; both the chicken egg drop and the hot and sour are bright ways to begin a meal.

HUNAN AND PEKING GARDEN
1262 Old Orchard Center
(Manchester east of Woods Mill Road)
227-6445

>>

Cuisine: Chinese
Serves: Lunch and dinner, every day
Prices: Moderate to expensive
Credit Cards: All major
Dress: Informal
Reservations: Accepted
Handicap Access: Satisfactory
Separate No-Smoking Section: Yes

A large menu doesn't mean much in Chinese restaurants in St. Louis. Every restaurant has a large menu, and too many of them look as if they came from the same print shop. But things are a little different at the Hunan and Peking, where a real effort is made—usually successfully—to display some individuality.

After all, when the menu has asterisks noting, "a dish of no rush," I'm charmed.

The Hunan and Peking is high on any list of Chinese restaurants in the area, with standards to match the competition, plus specials that are truly special.

Appetizers show outstanding egg rolls and spring rolls, delicious dumplings, and some hot, homemade cucumber pickles that are a wondrous side dish.

Oysters or clams with black bean sauce lead the menu for imagination; the plump, fresh shellfish are cooked with their own liquid, bean curd, mushrooms, shredded pork, green onions, and other vegetables, all in a tangy black bean sauce.

Orange beef is wonderful, lemon chicken less so, and an old standby like moo shu pork is a nice blend of textures and flavors served in delicate, delicious rice pancakes.

254

JEREMIAH'S
131 West Argonne
(West of Lindbergh,
Downtown Kirkwood)
821-2434

Cuisine: American
Serves: Dinner, Tuesday–Saturday; lunch, Tuesday–Friday
Prices: Moderate to expensive
Credit Cards: All major
Dress: Informal
Reservations: Accepted
Handicap Access: Satisfactory
Separate No-Smoking Section: Yes

The community of Kirkwood isn't known as a great dining area, but Jeremiah's has settled in nicely in a building just across from the railroad station, bringing pleasant meals to the heart of a community that is primarily residential.

Jeremiah's offers simple meals, usually a little on the bland side, but preparation is careful and service is brisk. It's just a most pleasant, calm place to dine.

Homemade soups are superior, and a summertime favorite of gazpacho is a proper blend of vegetables and tomatoes, though I found it underspiced.

Home cooking often gets a bad name, but Jeremiah's does dishes like liver and onions in superior style, and on the fancier side, individual beef Wellingtons are excellent. Top-quality liver is dredged lightly in a little flour, then sautéd with sweet onions so that the flavors blend and the liver remains juicy and tender. The Wellington is cooked on the rare side, with a tasty layer of mushrooms between the meat and the light pastry crust.

Fresh seafood, nicely prepared, is usually available as well.

A superb twice-baked potato heads the vegetable list. There's a modest wine list, and some superior desserts, especially a pecan-chocolate chip pie that simply sings.

JOHN MINEO'S
13490 Clayton Rd.
(At Mason)
434-5244

Cuisine: Italian
Serves: Dinner, Monday–Saturday
Prices: Expensive
Credit Cards: All major
Dress: Jackets required for men
Reservations: Accepted
Handicap Access: Satisfactory
Separate No-Smoking Section: Yes

It sometimes seems that you can stand almost anywhere in the St. Louis area, throw a stone in any direction and, if your arm is only slightly above average, you'll hit a fine Italian restaurant.

In the central part of the West County, you'll hit John Mineo's warm, comfortable establishment—another site where an alumnus of Tony's opened his own place, worked diligently and skillfully, and became successful.

John Mineo runs a stylish restaurant. He's usually on hand to deal with problems, make suggestions, and see that all the diners are comfortable, which is the prime task of a good restaurateur. He's also responsible for the touches that turn ordinary dishes into superior ones: a light hand with garlic here, a twist of the pepper mill there, and a squeeze of lemon juice somewhere else.

Pastas are outstanding here—from the fat, beautifully stuffed canneloni to the thin, elegant linguine or cappellini. Sauces show an imaginative touch and a loving hand. Veal, beef, chicken, and fish entrees reflect the same kitchen style, and simple grilled steaks are outstanding in every respect.

The wine list is lengthy, with a good collection of superior bottles and a nice Italian representation.

KREIS'

535 South Lindbergh Blvd.
(North of Conway Road)
993-0735

Cuisine: American, with German overtones
Serves: Dinner, every day
Prices: Moderate to expensive
Credit Cards: All major
Dress: Informal
Reservations: Accepted and advised
Handicap Access: Satisfactory
Separate No-Smoking Section: No

Given the transitory nature of the business, the fact that a restaurant has been in the same place for 45 years has to be considered a major recommendation.

Once Jack Kane's Kreis' and the record-holder for apostrophes, the venerable, warm establishment on Lindbergh Boulevard, eventually became just Kreis', and even when it went under the flag of the Tompras family, it survived the ownership change, and a subsequent fire, without shock to eyes, ears, or palate.

The bar area is larger, with more tables, and the rest rooms have been remodeled to fit handicap standards. But the large back room seems the same as it always was, with the paintings and the waiters aging gracefully.

Kreis' has a large and loyal clientele, making reservations vital almost any night, and the menu hasn't changed appreciably over the years. It's an old-fashioned, meat-and-potatoes restaurant, with large portions and good values. Basic steaks, chops, and roast beef lead the way, with some German dishes and a superlative fried catfish.

The wine list is about the same too, despite my comment that it was "unfit for a major restaurant." When I next visited, a year or so later, the manager had a sheepish smile as he handed me the list, reminded me of my criticism, and added, "I guess you'll say it again."

It's a little better today, but still not what a major restaurant should have.

The appetizer list is minimal, with toasted ravioli from the freezer and pickled herring from the jar. Soups are homemade, however, and are generally outstanding. Salads are satisfactory.

Entrees are what makes Kreis' a standout, however. The prime rib is a giant cut, nicely prepared, and the porterhouse steak is a winner, with the rich, hearty flavor that the best of all steaks should boast. Fried chicken is tasty, and the catfish, with a splendid cornmeal batter, is perfectly cooked so that the fish is at the peak of flavor.

Among the German dishes, sauerbraten shows a nice, tangy marinade and the schnitzel is satisfactory. Potato pancakes are heavy but flavorful.

Vegetables are adequate, and so are desserts, with strudel that is sometimes more like bread pudding with apples. For the meat-and-potatoes diner, there are few more satisfactory restaurants.

MASSA'S RESTAURANT

210 North Kirkwood Rd. (Lindbergh Blvd.)
(Kirkwood) 965-8050

15310 Manchester Rd. (Ballwin) 391-3700
75 Forum Center
Olive and Woods Mill (Creve Coeur) 878-1274
4120 North Lindbergh Blvd. (Bridgeton) 739-3894

Cuisine: Italian
Serves: Dinner, Monday–Saturday
Prices: Inexpensive to moderate
Credit Cards: All major
Dress: Informal
Reservations: Accepted, except for Friday and Saturday
Handicap Access: Passable
Separate No-Smoking Section: No

Long before there were green highway signs and numbers preceded by *I*, there was Lindbergh Boulevard, which wandered around St. Louis County in a long, leisurely loop. At that time, it served not only as a highway but also as a dividing line between the end of the civilized world and the place where fire-breathing dragons lived.

Today, it's known in various areas as U.S. 50, 61 and 67, and in the city of Kirkwood, it's called Kirkwood Road. That's why it's difficult to tell people how to get to Massa's in Kirkwood, because it's on North Kirkwood Road, which also is South Lindbergh Boulevard.

Maybe there ought to be a law against communities suddenly changing the names of streets at their borders, or even worse, in the middle of town, but that's another story and we were, after all, talking about Massa's. Besides, I'm told that the residents of

Kirkwood changed the name in angry response to some of Charles Lindbergh's pro-Nazi activities in the days before World War II.

There are four Massa's, or maybe the plural is Massa'ses, and the food is similar, but I prefer the one in Kirkwood because it has a slightly larger menu and a much larger wine list. In addition, I've lived in St. Louis more than 35 years, so I can find it.

There are beef, chicken, veal, and fish entrees, plus pizza and pasta, in large portions with tasty, fresh sauces. Some of the fried dishes tend to be overdone.

Cheese-garlic bread is a successful, if filling, appetizer, while crab Rangoon and fried mushrooms suffer from too much and too tough batter. Spinach salad is first rate, with sliced hard-boiled egg a nice touch.

Beef tenderloins are good. Pasta carbonara displays a rich bacon-mushroom sauce but misses the scrambled eggs. Pizza shows a wide variety of available toppings on a thin, crisp crust.

The best thing about Massa's is the lengthy, modestly priced wine list, and the chance to drink some splendid red wines at prices that are real bargains. Massa's list is especially heavy with full-bodied reds, which makes the manager a man after my own heart, and palate.

Service is smooth, and if you are still hungry after a full meal, cheesecake is a pleasant dessert.

PACIFIC SHORE CAFE
326 West Port Plaza
(I-270 and Page Boulevard)
434-1940

❖❖

Cuisine: General American, plus sushi bar
Serves: Dinner, every day; lunch, Monday–Friday
Prices: Moderate to expensive
Credit Cards: All major
Dress: Casual
Reservations: Accepted
Handicap Access: Satisfactory
Separate No-Smoking Section: No

The West Port Plaza complex, in west St. Louis County, brings together office buildings, a couple of hotels, boutique shops, movie theaters, and lots of restaurants and bars. The plaza is built in a sort of mock-Swiss village design and offers little that is truly distinguished.

The restaurants are on the ordinary side, except for the Pacific Shore Cafe, a casual spot that is part traditional steak-and-seafood house, part singles bar—and part sushi bar.

The sushi bar is excellent, and as anyone who has read this far certainly knows, I'm weak for sushi. I love the flavors and textures of the various fish, and the slightly vinegary rice that comes with them. Even the fiery green horseradish, in tiny amounts, is a pleasing addition, and the ginger slices are special. Watching a good sushi chef at work is exciting; the knife and hand movements are beautiful, and the final presentation looks like a work of art.

The selection varies with the season, but my weakness for sushi inevitably leaves my stomach filled and my pockets empty.

The menu shows many other appetizers, both Asiatic and American, like oysters and clams on the half-shell, skewered and

262

grilled chicken, soft-shell crabs, smelts, fried squid in a delicious and delicate tempura-style batter, and other delicacies.

Baby back ribs are barbecued in what the menu calls "Hawaiian style" and are meaty, tender, and juicy; they are brushed—not soaked—in a light, flavorful, slightly piquant soy-and-ginger sauce. Excellent ribs.

Marinated, grilled tuna is outstanding, as are traditional Japanese tempura-battered shrimp and vegetables. Some of the broiled fish seems slightly overdone, and vegetables tend to be overcooked, or cold, or both.

The wine list is too small, but a careful search can turn up a satisfactory bottle or two.

PATRICK'S

342 West Port Plaza
(I-270 at Page Blvd.) **878-6767**

1308 Clayton-Clarkson Center
Clarkson Road (south of U.S. 40) **256-3560**

❖❖

Cuisine: Modern American
Serves: Lunch and dinner, every day
Prices: Moderate to expensive
Credit Cards: All major
Dress: Casual
Reservations: Accepted
Handicap Access: Satisfactory
Separate No-Smoking Section: Yes

Modern American is the style at both of these bright, trendy restaurants, where the fare covers the world, mostly calmed down for American palates.

They're popular with family groups, with a mix-and-match menu that offers seafood, Mexican, and Asiatic dishes, good salads and large portions.

Service and presentation are good, but the kitchens don't always seem as careful as they might be.

The menus are similar, and the best bet usually is fresh fish, grilled or broiled in a simple manner. Sauces often detract rather than enhance. As a general rule, simple is better in terms of most items.

They're pleasant, serve nourishing meals that are good values, but fall short of excellence.

PUEBLO NUEVO
7401 North Lindbergh Blvd.
(North of I-270)
831-6885

❖❖❖

Cuisine: Mexican
Serves: Lunch and dinner, Monday–Saturday
Prices: Inexpensive to moderate
Credit Cards: MC, V
Dress: Casual
Reservations: Not accepted
Handicap Access: Passable (difficult when crowded)
Separate No-Smoking Section: No

Ever since it opened, in the spring of 1984, Pueblo Nuevo has been my favorite among Mexican restaurants in the area. Every time I visit, the menu is a little larger, or familiar dishes show delightful variations. It just keeps getting better.

A tiny, brightly lighted storefront in the North County, Pueblo Nuevo offers a wide selection of freshly prepared, nicely seasoned dishes, many not part of the usual "Mexican- American" menu.

Most items are rather mild, showing the flavor of meat and herbs properly combined and cooked. Hot sauce—actually two hot sauces in squeeze bottles—is available. The light red is adequate, but without much character. But the dark red is superior and powerful, rich and tangy, with a hint of chocolate.

Guacamole is a proper starter for dinner, and Pueblo Nuevo makes it without a blender. The avocado is delicately forked until slightly lumpy, contributing a robust texture and flavor and, equally important, not drowned in mayonnaise. It's bolstered with a few—not too many—tomatoes, and has a delightful peppery-garlicky backtaste.

Other splendid appetizers include chorizo sausage and melted

265

cheese that, when put atop a chip, makes nachos far better than those served anywhere else. Real nachos, laden with beans, beef, sour cream, and jalapeño peppers, are a meal in themselves. And chicharrones, or pork rinds, are greasy and delicious, and you can feel those arteries clog as you munch.

Removing Pueblo Nuevo from the ordinary are entrees like carne ranchera, or roast pork in a delicious red sauce, and birria, or goat, stewed and served with fresh, warm tortillas and beans. The goat is tender, slightly stringy like beef brisket, and delicious. Pozole, a chicken-pork-hominy stew, also is a winner. All the dishes are tangy; none of them burn. Add hot sauce if you like fire.

Cornmeal enchiladas are my favorite, filled with beef or chicken and topped with a piquant sauce and a dollop of sour cream. Flautas, or fried enchiladas, are good, too. Burritos, made of wheat flour, are satisfactory, and so are tacos. Empanadas also are winners, with the crisp, tender pastry crust showing a hint of sweetness that contrasts beautifully with the spiced meat inside.

The tamale is heavy with corn meal and extremely filling; refried beans, with a hint of bacon grease, are delicious, and hot sauce makes them even better.

House wine is available, but I prefer the Mexican beers: especially Dos Equis among the dark, Carta Blanca among the light, and rich and flavorful Pacifico, with lots of hops. Corona is too much like watery American beers for my taste.

Bread pudding is an outstanding dessert—light and yet rich with raisins and cinnamon. The sopapillas and flan are also very tasty.

ROBATA OF JAPAN
Gold Tower Building
111 West Port Plaza
I-270 at Page
434-1007

❖-❖

Cuisine: Japanese
Serves: Dinner, every day; lunch, Monday–Friday
Prices: Moderate to expensive
Credit Cards: All major
Dress: Informal
Reservations: Accepted and advised
Handicap Access: Satisfactory
Separate No-Smoking Section: No

Those who like their food entertaining, or their entertainment filling, will find Robata a proper place.

Dinner is the show, with a handy chef chopping and slicing and cutting with rat-a-tat-rhythm and uncommon skill as he works at a large grill that is three-fourths surrounded by seats and an eating area for eight diners.

The chef juggles knives and spatulas, and in the midst of all that, he prepares a satisfactory dinner of sukiyaki, a mixture of meat and vegetables prepared on the grill while you watch. It's nicely seasoned, and very tasty.

Japanese specialties stand out. Fried shrimp and vegetables, in a feather-light, very tasty tempura batter, are exceptional. There are a couple of non-Japanese dishes, but they're generally not up to the same standards.

One small drawback is that while the dining experience is enjoyable, the eight-person seating arrangement makes Robata a very difficult place for a cozy tête-a-tête.

267

S & P OYSTER CO.

14501 Manchester at Baxter Road
(Ballwin) **256-3300**

Highway 94 south of I-70
(St. Charles) **947-3300**

Highway 159 south of St. Clair Square
(Fairview Heights, IL) **618-234-3300**

◆◆

Cuisine: Seafood
Serves: Lunch and dinner, every day
Prices: Moderate to expensive
Credit Cards: All major
Dress: Informal
Reservations: Accepted
Handicap Access: Satisfactory
Separate No-Smoking Section: Yes

Inexpensive lobsters and oysters are the big items at these large, relaxed, moderately priced seafood restaurants. The lobsters are what Nor'Easterners call "chicken lobsters," or the one-pound variety, and the oysters come from the Gulf, but they're tasty, nicely prepared and draw customers.

The first edition of this guide listed only the West County operation. Since then, others have opened in St. Charles County and in Illinois near Fairview Heights.

The S & P group, like seafood operations all over the country, has benefited from two concurrent factors, the leap in seafood interest among American diners and the lower prices and better service offered by air freight companies.

There's a lot of greenery, and a large patio, at the West County restaurant, and there's also a lot of fresh seafood, properly prepared.

Oysters on the half shell are the major appetizer, as they should be, and a nice touch is the placement of all the cocktail sauce fixin's on the table so that a personal blend of ketchup, horseradish, Tabasco, and Worcestershire sauce can be designed. Personally, I think a squirt of lemon and a drop or two of Tabasco is all an oyster needs, or perhaps some shallot vinegar.

Appetizers also include some splendid gumbo, nicely spiced and filled with shrimp, vegetables, and sausage, and pretty good spiced shrimp, plus a variety of other items to whet the appetite. Broiled oysters topped with Swiss cheese don't work, however, because the cheese flavor overpowers the delicate bivalve.

S & P's lobsters are steamed just right, arriving piping hot, tender, juicy and so succulent they're almost sweet. There are various lobster bargains, and whether at a discount or at full price, the lobsters are winners.

Fried oysters are prepared in a delicious cornmeal batter, and soft fish, like flounder, are broiled to the perfect point, where the fish is juicy and succulent.

The nonfish eater—a growing rarity in the America of the 1990s—can have steaks or chicken, and there are a few Cajun-style items, but nothing matches the simple grilled fish.

The wine list is modest, but has sufficient variety and proper pricing, and the Key lime pie is all the dessert anyone needs.

TACHIBANA
12967 Olive Blvd.
(At Fee Fee Road)
434-3455

❖❖❖

Cuisine: Japanese
Serves: Dinner, Tuesday–Sunday; lunch, Tuesday–Friday
Prices: Moderate to expensive
Credit Cards: All major
Dress: Informal
Reservations: Accepted
Handicap Access: Satisfactory
Separate No-Smoking Section: Yes

There's something about Japanese cooking that makes it an art form, or show business, as well as an elegant preparation of food. The chefs at Robata juggle and twirl and chop with a toe- tapping rhythm. At Tachibana, sushi chefs have the same touch, cutting fresh fish into identical slices, molding damp, cooked, cold rice into small rectangular chunks, dabbing it with the tiniest bit of fiery green horseradish, then making fish and rice into a delightful appetizer.

The wide-ranging Japanese menu includes a superior sushi bar and a large number of traditional dishes, plus some simple grilled selections for the less experimental diner.

As described, sushi involves raw fish with rice. Sashimi, also available, takes the same fish, in slices of about the same size, served without rice. Both usually have that fiery horseradish and wonderful pickled ginger, to be taken as desired.

There are other appetizers, however, like teriyaki-flavored shrimp wrapped with bacon and grilled, which is a wonderful dish. And teriyaki chicken, served on a skewer, is properly marinated, tender, and juicy. The Japanese cucumber salad, or sunomuno, is a delicious accompaniment—light and palate-cleansing. Miso soup, a clear-to-brownish bean soup with a few bits of tofu and some green onions, is outstanding.

Sukiyaki, a brilliant blend of beef, vegetables, bean curd, soy sauce, and beef stock, cooked at tableside, is a lovely dish, with all the flavors curling up together in marvelous style. A deep-fried pork cutlet is less satisfactory, but simple broiled salmon or chicken, brushed with teriyaki sauce, are superior entrees.

Classic tempura, that marvelous, light batter that makes a shrimp a wondrous thing, is usually outstanding. I'm very fond of the fried vegetables, too, with a single mushroom, or a slice of sweet potato or eggplant, becoming something quite special. And there are few onion rings in the world to compare with those in a tempura batter.

Sake and beer are the most popular drinks, along with tea, and there are several desserts and the ubiquitous fortune cookies, too.

THE VILLAGE BAR
12247 Manchester
(Just East of Ballas Road)
821-4532

Cuisine: Hamburgers, American bar food
Serves: Lunch and dinner, Monday–Saturday (same menu)
Prices: Inexpensive
Credit Cards: None
Dress: Casual
Reservations: Not applicable
Handicap Access: Difficult (narrow passageway)
Separate No-Smoking Section: No

Before there were fern bars and sports bars, there were bars like the Village Bar, where shuffleboard was the participant activity, several sets provided televised sports, and a small grill brought forth great hamburgers and out-of-this world onion rings.

The flat grill at the Village is different from the open charcoal grill used, say, at O'Connell's—and the results are different, too. The flat grill retains more grease, so the burger has a different flavor, lacking the charred crispness the other grill provides.

But there are times when the grease quotient needs help, and that's when the Village Bar is perfect. There are ordinary hamburgers and what they call a "better burger," slightly larger, topped with Swiss cheese and sweet raw onion, served on a small kaiser roll with poppy seeds. Both are glorious.

The Village Bar also is one of the very few restaurants that slices and batters its own onions, then cooks them in fresh grease. The result is an onion ring that is sweet, tender, and practically melts in the mouth. Once you've eaten them here, the prebattered, frozen onion rings that are so common will never again satisfy.

There are other traditional bar sandwiches, soups, rather ordinary chili, and some lunch specials served by a capable, relaxed staff. The lunch crowd is mixed, with both ties and overalls in evidence.

Make no mistake: the Village Bar is primarily a bar, albeit a friendly one, but it's worth the journey for a hamburger and some onion rings.

LET'S TAKE A RIDE

❖❖❖

Wandering farther afield in Missouri, plus Belleville, Fairview Heights, and other nearby Illinois communities.

Andria's, O'Fallon, Illinois
Franco's, Belleville, Illinois
Hunter's Hollow, Labadie, Missouri
Malmaison, St. Alban's, Missouri
Mother-in-Law House, St. Charles, Missouri
Vintage 1847, Hermann, Missouri

ANDRIA'S
6805 Old Collinsville Rd.
East of I-64
O'Fallon, Illinois
618-632-4866

⫸⫸

Cuisine: Steaks, other traditional American
Serves: Dinner, Monday–Saturday
Prices: Moderate to expensive
Credit Cards: MC, V
Dress: Informal
Reservations: Accepted, Monday–Thursday only, and advised
Handicap Access: Entrance satisfactory, rest rooms difficult
Separate No-Smoking Section: No

The parent to Sam's Steaks (see South section), Andria's earned its own solid reputation as a superior place for steaks and chops in what used to be a country house before urbanization and Fairview Heights closed in on it. Outstanding raw material, prepared simply and well, is the secret to a long and successful run that proved frills and fancies are unnecessary.

The restaurant, in a white frame house that sits in a tree-lined grove, is about 20 to 30 minutes from downtown St. Louis, east of the Fairview Heights shopping center. It's busy, and long waits can be common on weekend nights. Once inside, there's sometimes a cramped feeling of tables too close together.

Andria's is a restaurant for the hearty eater who wants to concentrate on the main course; steaks and chops are large, and the only appetizer is an excellent soup of the day. There's a salad bar, not my favorite dining idea (if I wanted to carry my own food, I'd have stayed in the Army), but I know a lot of people like them. The selection is modest, but enough to create a proper dinner salad, and dressings are pleasant.

Steaks include sirloin of two sizes and a delicious tenderloin, and there's also prime rib, sautéd chicken breast, catfish, a fish of the day, and one or two other items. An outstanding baked potato comes alongside, wrapped in brown paper (not that repulsive foil) and well cooked so that the inside is mealy and filled with flavor. French fries, cut thick and freshly prepared, are also splendid.

The pork chop and the beef tenderloin are brilliant; both are large and grilled perfectly. The chop is rich and delicious, with the hint of sweetness that great pork will demonstrate, and the steak is tender and succulent. The prime rib and the sirloin were less than a half-step behind. Catfish, served in a filet, was very tasty, with a fine cornmeal batter, and the hush puppies that accompanied it were delicious.

Desserts are satisfactory, but after a meal at Andria's, one rarely has room.

FRANCO'S
7000 West Main St.
Belleville, Illinois
618-397-6886

❖❖❖

Cuisine: Italian
Serves: Dinner, Monday–Saturday; lunch, Tuesday–Friday
Prices: Inexpensive to moderate
Credit Cards: MC, V
Dress: Informal
Reservations: Accepted only to 6:30 p.m.
Handicap Access: Satisfactory
Separate No-Smoking Section: Yes

Long before their son opened his own restaurant, discussed in the Downtown section of this book, Franco's was a bustling little family-style restaurant on the Illinois side of the river, first in Cahokia, now in Belleville, some 20 minutes east of downtown St. Louis.

Franco Sanfilippo and his wife, Concetta, do exemplary things in their kitchen, and everything is homemade and freshly prepared, which adds a special touch.

The style is Sicilian, with lots of tomatoes and garlic, and plenty of black olives and capers, too.

Franco's caponata and pepperonata are as good as anything to accompany a predinner anywhere. The former is based on roasted eggplant, the latter on sweet peppers. Once cooked, they're chopped and mixed with garlic—lots of garlic—capers, olive oil, olives, and some splendid spices, then served chilled. They're perfect with chunks of Italian bread.

Speaking of bread, Franco's also serves a garlic-cheese bread that will destroy an appetite faster than anything I know. When dining at Franco's, by the way, it's vital that people who will be sharing a car on the ride home share the garlic, or like each other a lot, or someone will have to walk.

Pastas come in all sizes and shapes, all perfectly complemented by rich, hearty sauces. Penne with onions, bacon, and tomatoes is wondrous, and linguine with seafood is a winner.

Entrees include shrimp in a dark, tangy marinara sauce that's as good as any around, and beef and fish dishes are beautifully prepared. A couple of daily specials augment the regular menu.

Portions are huge, and there's a small wine list that has some tasty Italian varieties—I tend to have a weakness for Chianti and Barolo when pasta is on the plate.

Difficult as it may be, one should save room for dessert because Mrs. Sanfilippo's pastries are magnificent, especially the cannoli, whose flaky, light crust contains a delicious, but not overly sweet, ricotta mixture.

HUNTER'S HOLLOW
Front Street
Labadie, Missouri
458-3326, 742-2279

❖❖❖

Cuisine: Country French, American overtones, barbecue on weekends
Serves: Lunch and dinner, Tuesday–Sunday
Prices: Moderate to expensive
Credit Cards: MC, V
Dress: Informal
Reservations: Accepted, strongly advised on weekends
Handicap Access: Satisfactory (few steps at entrance)
Separate No-Smoking Section: Yes

We've all had meals so delicious and filling that the only proper tribute was a nap. At Hunter's Hollow, where the meals are just about that good, there are now a few bedrooms, and since Hunter's Hollow is in beautiful downtown Labadie, Missouri, there really isn't much to do after dinner except turn down the sheets.

Labadie is a wide spot on a country road, with a main street that's a block long on one side, half a block on the other. Don Wolfsberger brought it into being in 1987 with a restaurant that has been attracting people ever since. Woods surround Labadie, and the Missouri River is close by, though there's a massive Union Electric plant that blocks access to the river itself.

Hunter's Hollow has bloomed into a splendid restaurant, serving a fine blend of Country French and American cuisine. The ride is pretty too. It's about an hour from downtown St. Louis, along Highway 100 (Manchester Road) to Highway T, then up hill and down dale to Labadie.

Highway T is unmarked. A sign says "Lewis and Clark Trail," but if you miss it, don't panic. A few miles farther is the little town of Gray Summit. Turn right and follow the road past the Ralston Purina farms; it leads to Labadie. If you miss Gray Summit and hit I-44, you've gone too far.

The menu is simple: a few steaks, a rack of lamb, chicken, cornish hen, Missouri trout, pheasant, home-smoked meats, and a few daily specials. But Chef Claude Courtoisier adds the extra touch, the additional herb for impressive results.

Onion marmalade does splendid things to chicken liver pâté, for example, and some pistachio nuts are a gorgeous addition to a creamy curry sauce. On one visit, the vegetable was salsify, rarely seen on local tables, but a delicious accompaniment and a nice change from the ubiquitous broccoli and cauliflower. Speaking of vegetables, white asparagus is served on spring evenings—a rare treat.

Another outstanding appetizer is a salmon-shrimp roll, served with delicious curry mayonnaise, and both a Caesar and a spinach salad were first-rate.

The entrees followed suit, with a light, tangy curry sauce a delight on sautéd scallops, and a rubbing with rosemary highlighting the cornish hen. Pheasant with apples and green peppercorn sauce is deservedly popular, and a simple filet, topped with a handful of morel mushrooms, was perfectly grilled.

The wine list is strong, with good vintages and labels at moderate prices, and desserts are highlighted by a strawberry whipped cream cake. Chocolate mousse falls short.

MALMAISON
St. Alban's, Missouri
458-0131

∗∗∗

Cuisine: Country French, with eclectic overtones
Serves: Lunch and dinner, Wednesday–Sunday
Prices: Expensive to very expensive
Credit Cards: All major
Dress: Informal (jackets preferred)
Reservations: Accepted, advised on weekends
Handicap Access: Entrance satisfactory, rest rooms very difficult
(stairs)
Separate No-Smoking Area: Yes

Gilbert and Simone Andujar have operated several successful French restaurants in the area—he's out front, she's usually in the kitchen, though she bounds exuberantly through the dining room from time to time, embracing old friends, and making new ones as she goes.

The restaurant, in a charming rural setting, can provide an exemplary dining experience. It's about an hour from downtown, via Missouri 100 (Manchester Road in the West County) to Highway T, which wanders through the woods for a while, then comes practically to the front door.

The Andujars are from southern France, so there are lovely Provençal and Marseilles gifts to the cuisine, but also touches of Italian and even Cajun cooking. Classic French, on the lighter side, involves some brilliant hollandaise sauce, and roast duck in the old- fashioned style, well done with a crisp skin and a perfect green peppercorn sauce that adds a little tang but no unpleasant heat.

Among the appetizers, escargot are prepared as well as I've ever tasted, with a little Pernod adding a slight anise overtone that gives the dish a splendid flavor. Onion soup, with caramelized onions, is hearty, and stuffed mushrooms are splendid.

Given the country site, the Andjuars raise a few of their own vegetables, and nothing is better than a fresh, vine-ripe tomato, sliced with some endive and a light vinaigrette dressing. That's for summer, of course, when tomatoes are local and spectacular; the rest of the year, they should be ignored.

Fresh salmon, poached and served with that perfect hollandaise, is a superb entree, and liver and onions, with a hint of vinegar in the sauce, is another winning dish. Salmon can be grilled, though I think poaching—if it's timed right—is better. Roast duck, veal in several different sauces, sweetbreads, and other entrees are all prepared stylishly.

Desserts are led by Simone Andjuar's specialty—an almond cookie basket filled with fresh fruit and ice cream—and it's an outstanding signature dish. Chocolate mousse is good, but not quite dark enough for my taste, and sabayon, the French version of zabaglione, is light and tasty.

There's a good-sized wine list, with a fine selection of French offerings, but I found prices, especially among the imports, on the high side.

Malmaison (the name of the home of Napoleon's Josephine) is a charming restaurant, with a large fireplace for winter, and a lovely patio for al fresco dining in nice weather, when one can smell the roses growing nearby.

MOTHER-IN-LAW HOUSE
500 South Main St.
St. Charles, Missouri
946-9444

Cuisine: American
Serves: Dinner, Tuesday–Saturday; lunch, Monday–Saturday
Prices: Moderate
Credit Cards: All major
Dress: Informal
Reservations: Accepted
Handicap Access: Passable (few steps at entrance)
Separate No-Smoking Section: Yes

The rehabbed "Old Town" district of St. Charles, the state's first capital, involves several blocks of brick-paved streets lined with antique shops, boutiques, and restaurants—nice for strolling on a nice-weather evening.

Cuisine is secondary to charmingly cute in most of the neighborhood restaurants, including the Mother-in-Law House, in a 125-year-old brick building decorated in a semi-Victorian style.

The menu is basic American—roast beef, fried chicken, a steak or two, Missouri trout, and a couple of specials. There's a salad bar built around a beam in the middle of the dining room; it's delightfully country and old-fashioned. There are greens, of course, with several dressings, but I prefer the pickled beets, marinated cucumbers, chilled creamed peas, and macaroni salad, with real elbow macaroni, and none of your fancy pastas. Water chestnuts wrapped in crisp bacon also are a pleasant appetizer.

Fresh, delicious blueberry muffins are served throughout the meal and are a high spot. Prime rib and fried chicken are passable, but undistinguished, and without great flavor. The same goes for the baked potatoes.

Homemade desserts are a specialty, beginning with the coconut cream pie that reportedly comes from the recipe of owner Donna Hafer's own mother-in-law. It's tall and handsome, with a superior crust and excellent coconut cream on top, but the custard in the middle was slightly gummy and should have been creamier.

Service is pleasant, and the room is a kind of throwback to dining rooms in rural America a century ago.

VINTAGE 1847
Stone Hill Winery
Hermann, Missouri
486-3479

❖❖

Cuisine: American
Serves: Lunch and dinner, every day
Prices: Moderate to expensive
Credit Cards: MC, V
Dress: Informal
Reservations: Accepted, vital on weekends
Handicap Access: Entrance satisfactory, steps to rest rooms
Separate No-Smoking Section: No

Before California even had statehood, they were producing wine in Hermann, Missouri. German immigrants settled in this Missouri River town, about 70 miles west of St. Louis, in the 1820s and '30s, and began growing grapes and making wine almost immediately.

The Vintage 1847, on the grounds of the Stone Hill Winery, honors the first wine to be made on the site. The winery's main building, next door, is a national landmark, and its cellars hold some of the state's best wines.

The restaurant is in a converted barn, with stalls turned into oversized booths, and high ceilings bringing a pleasant aura.

During Prohibition, by the way, the winery was closed and the cellars were turned over to mushroom growing. There was a major cleanup task when wine's time came again.

The winery tour is interesting and whets the appetite, and the Vintage 1847 sells winery products. It also boasts one of the nation's most unusual menus. Chef Gary Buckler's spiral bound volume is both menu and cookbook, giving the diner the chance to discover exactly what goes into each dish, and if you like it, you can buy the book on the way out. If Buckler is around, he'll autograph it.

And it's an outstanding restaurant, with American fare heightened by a few French overtones. Fresh meats and produce show outstanding flavor under Buckler's careful, imaginative, loving touch.

Rough, beautifully textured, homemade country pâtés are elegant appetizers, and soups are rich and hearty. The quiche is as good as any I've ever sampled.

Steaks and chops are delicious, and the roast duck is something special—with crisp, tasty skin. Missouri trout and catfish have the wonderful flavor provided by freshness. Buckler has a fine sense of sauces, and he uses fresh vegetables from neighboring farms as accompaniments.

All the Stone Hill wines are available, including an excellent sparkling wine as an aperitif. For a rich red in the Rhone style, try the Norton, from a native American grape and probably the best red wine made in Missouri. It needs age, however, so don't get a young one, and it's expensive, but worth it. On the lighter side, Seyval and Vidal are fine dry whites.

Desserts are worth waiting for, some superior fruit pies in season, and pecan pies to make you weep.

Hermann is about a 90-minute drive from St. Louis, via I-70 and south on Missouri 19 or, staying on the south side of the Missouri River, via I-44 and Missouri 100 through Washington. It's a lovely trip on a spring or fall day.

Alphabetical Index

289

Cuisine Index

292

About the Author

Joe Pollack has been writing for the *St. Louis Post Dispatch* for nearly 20 years. In addition to his "Dining Out" column, he writes a wine column, theater and movie criticism, and general features. He is also a theater and movie critic for KMOV-TV in St. Louis. The father of three daughters, he lives in St. Louis, which he affectionately calls "the city that feeds him."